TOPS & TOES™

A Whimsical Collection to Delight Hat & Sock Knitters

EDITED BY KARA GOTT WARNER

HOUSE of
WHITE
BIRCHES
PUBLISHERS
SINCE 1947

TOPS & TOES™

EDITOR	Kara Gott Warner
ART DIRECTOR	Brad Snow
PUBLISHING SERVICES DIRECTOR	Brenda Gallmeyer
MANAGING EDITOR	Dianne Schmidt
ASSISTANT ART DIRECTOR	Nick Pierce
COPY SUPERVISOR	Michelle Beck
COPY EDITOR	Amanda Ladig
TECHNICAL EDITOR	Charlotte Quiggle
TECHNICAL ARTIST	Nicole Gage
GRAPHIC ARTS SUPERVISOR	Ronda Bechinski
GRAPHIC ARTISTS	Jessi Butler, Minette Collins Smith
PRODUCTION ASSISTANTS	Marj Morgan, Judy Neuenschwander
PHOTOGRAPHY SUPERVISOR	Tammy Christian
PHOTOGRAPHY	Scott Campbell
PHOTO STYLIST	Martha Coquat

Printed in China
First Printing: 2009
Library of Congress Number: 2008901111
Hardcover ISBN: 978-1-59217-220-7
Softcover ISBN: 978-1-59217-233-7

DRGbooks.com

1 2 3 4 5 6 7 8 9

WELCOME!

When it comes to knitting hats and socks, there's such a world of excitement to be found in these small, compact creations. We've selected a variety of designs to excite sock fanatics, as well as an assortment of colorful caps to keep those eager hands busy for hours to come.

In this book, you'll find three easy-to-navigate sections: *Tops, Toes and Sets*. In the front of the book, you will find an extensive *Special Techniques* section that we're sure you'll consider an invaluable resource. If you're a newcomer to sock knitting, this section will help you understand each technique, step-by-step. If you're a more seasoned knitter, you may pick up a new way of working a familiar technique.

In the *Tops* section, you'll be impressed by the variety of hat patterns for babies, kids and adults. These projects are simple, cleverly creative and approachable for knitters of every level. Need to make a gift on the fly? The *Spring Has Sprung Hat*, made in stockinette stitch with appliquéd flower accents, makes for the perfect last-minute gift, sure to impress everyone.

Need to add a little excitement to those feet? We've selected some unexpected approaches to the basic sock shape in our *Toes* selections. For the new sock knitter, the *Simple Self-Striping Socks* make the perfect first project. Or, add some pep to your step with the *Playful Polka Dot Socks*.

If you need to find the perfect shower gift, our *Sets* collection offers a generous selection of matching hat and sock patterns. For a girl or a boy, the *Three Times a Charm Hat & Booties Set* is sure to inspire you. The cute ear flap hat and matching booties are designed using interchangeable elements to really help you make this project one-of-a-kind.

So, pick up those needles, and start knitting some Tops & Toes!
Wishing you happy, fun-filled hours of knitting!

Kara Gott Warner, Editor

TOPS

TOES

SETS

TOPS

These delightfully small creations will make heads turn. Try your hand at projects ranging from fun shapes with splashes of color, to classically elegant styles. From start to finish a hat takes just a few days to complete, or sometimes even in hours. The projects to follow will inspire and excite you to get those needles moving!

Spring Has Sprung Hat

This adorable hat is inspired by the welcome sight of sprouting spring flowers.

DESIGN BY ANN SQUIRE

SIZES

Infant's 0–3 (3–6, 6–12, 12–18) months. Instructions are given for smallest size, with larger sizes in parentheses. When only 1 number is given, it applies to all sizes.

FINISHED MEASUREMENT

Circumference (unstretched): 10½ (13, 15, 17) inches

MATERIALS

- Mission Falls 1824 Wool (worsted weight; 100% superwash wool; 85 yds/50g per ball): 1 ball each mallow #025 (MC) and sprout #531 (CC) (Note: only a small amount of CC is needed)
- Size 6 (4mm) double-pointed needles (set of 4)
- Size 7 (4.5mm) double-pointed needles (set of 4) or size needed to obtain gauge
- Stitch markers, 1 in CC for beg of rnd
- An old felted sweater, craft felt, or similar non-fraying fabric

GAUGE

17 sts and 24 rows = 4 inches in St st with larger needles.
To save time, take time to check gauge.

PATTERN NOTE

The flowers that embellish the hat are cut from a wool sweater that has been felted. To do this, take an old 100 percent (non-superwash) wool sweater, put it through the "hot" cycle on your washing machine, and then place in the dryer. The sweater will become shrunken and felted and may be cut into decorative shapes without danger of fraying. If you prefer, you may use craft felt or another non-fraying fabric. Test for colorfastness by washing before use.

Hat

BODY

With smaller needles and MC, cast on 45 (54, 63, 72) sts. Distribute sts evenly on 3 dpns; place marker for beg of rnd and join, taking care not to twist sts.

Knit 6 rnds.

Change to larger needles and knit 7 rnds. Cut MC.

Join CC and knit 1 rnd, purl 2 rnds. Cut CC.

Join MC and knit 12 (13, 15, 17) rnds.
Next rnd: *K5 (6, 7, 8), place marker; rep from * around.

CROWN

Rnd 1: *Knit to 2 sts before marker, k2tog; rep from * around.
Rnd 2: Knit.

Rep [Rnds 1 and 2] 2 (3, 4, 5) times— 18 sts.
Next rnd: K2tog around, removing all markers—9 sts.
Next rnd: K2tog 4 times, k1—5 sts.

Cut yarn, leaving a 5-inch tail.

Using tapestry needle, thread tail through rem sts, pull tight then secure to WS.

Weave in all ends.

Place 4 pins evenly spaced around brim to mark points where flower stems are to be embroidered. Using CC and tapestry needle, and starting at green stripe, work 1 to 1½ inches of chain st to form stems. For each leaf, work a single large chain st diagonally out from base of stem. Using template cut 4 circles from felted sweater. Cut 5 small triangles from edge of each circle to form petals. Using a small amount of MC, CC or another yarn, sew flowers to hat at top of stems. If desired, use a French knot to decorate center of flowers. ✿

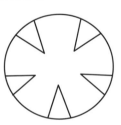

Flower Template

Chain Stitch

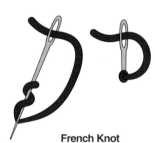

French Knot

All Buttoned Up Beanie

Calling all girls! This hat not only keeps her warm, but buttons up the back to show off that ponytail too!

DESIGN BY JULIE GADDY

SIZE

Fits child approx 7 years old to teen

FINISHED MEASUREMENT

Circumference (above cuff): 19½ inches

MATERIALS

- Plymouth Baby Alpaca Worsted Paint (worsted weight; 100% baby alpaca; 102 yds/50g per ball): 2 balls variegated pinks color #8818
- Size 5 (3.75mm) 16-inch circular needle
- Size 8 (5mm) double-pointed and 16-inch circular needles or size needed to obtain gauge
- Stitch markers, 1 in CC for beg of rnd
- 4 [⅞-inch] buttons
- Matching sewing thread

GAUGE

19 sts and 24 rnds = 4 inches/10cm in St st with larger needle.
To save time, take time to check gauge.

PATTERN STITCH

K1, P1 Rib (even number of sts)
Rnd 1: *K1, p1; rep from * around.
Rep Rnd 1 for pat.
Note: When working in rows, work the sts as they present themselves, i.e. knit the knit sts and purl the purl sts.

PATTERN NOTES

The cuff is worked in the round, then a button band is added and the body is worked back-and-forth for 3 inches, after which it is rejoined and finished in the round.

When working the crown, change to double-pointed needles when stitches no longer fit comfortably on circular needle.

Hat

CUFF

With smaller needle, cast on 96 sts; place marker and join, taking care not to twist sts.
Work K1, P1 Rib for 4 inches.

BODY

Row 1 (RS): With larger needle, work 8 sts in established rib (buttonhole band), k88; using backwards loop method, cast on 8 sts for button band, turn—104 sts.
Row 2 (WS): [P1, k1] 4 times, p88, work 8 sts in established rib.
Continuing to work 8 sts in rib at beg and end of row and 88 sts in St st, work 2 rows.
Buttonhole Row 1 (RS): K1, p1, bind off 2 sts, work in established pat to end.

Buttonhole Row 2: Work in established pat to bound off sts, cast on 3 sts, k1, p1. *Work in established pat for 1 inch, then work buttonhole rows again; rep from *. Work in established pat until hat measures approx 7 inches from beg, ending with a RS row.

Next row (WS): Bind off 8 sts in pat, work to end of row, turn—96 sts.

Joining rnd: With RS facing, knit all sts around, place marker for beg of rnd, and join, tucking bound off edge to inside of hat.

Work even in St st until hat measures 8 inches and on last rnd, place markers every 12 sts.

CROWN

Rnd 1 (dec): *Knit to 2 sts before marker, k2tog; rep from * around—88 sts.

Rnd 2: Knit.

Rep [Rnds 1 and 2] 7 times—32 sts.

Rep [Rnd 1] 3 times, removing markers on last rnd—8 sts.

Cut yarn leaving a 10 inch tail. Using tapestry needle, thread tail through rem sts, and pull tight, and secure to WS.

FINISHING

Sew 8 bound off sts of button band to underside of hat at top and bottom—it is directly under the buttonhole band. Sew buttons to button band, lining buttons up with button holes. Sew rem button to top of crown. Weave in all ends and block hat as desired. ✪

Itty Bitty Buggie Preemie Caps

Create a "buzz" making these fun and quick-to-knit preemie caps.

DESIGNS BY ERSSIE MAJOR

 **INTERMEDIATE**

SIZE
Preemie with 12-inch head circumference

FINISHED MEASUREMENTS
Circumference: 10 inches
Height: 5 inches (with brim unrolled)

MATERIALS
- Debbie Bliss Rialto Aran (worsted weight; 100% merino wool extra fine superwash; 88yds/50g per skein): Ladybug: 1 skein each ebony #15 (MC) and red #18 (CC); Butterfly: 1 skein each ebony #15 (MC) and purple #13 (CC) and small amount of gold #20; Bumblebee: 1 skein each ebony #15 (MC) and gold #20 (CC) See Pattern Notes
- Size 7 (4.5mm) double-pointed needles (set of 5) or size needed to obtain gauge
- 2 bobbins
- Stitch markers, 1 in CC for beg of rnd

GAUGE
19 sts and 28 rnds = 4 inches/10cm in St st. To save time, take time to check gauge.

SPECIAL ABBREVIATION
Increase 1 (Inc1): Knit in front and back of st.

SPECIAL TECHNIQUES
I-Cord: *K4, do not turn, slip sts back to LH needle; rep from * until cord is desired length. Bind off.

PATTERN NOTES
1 skein of ebony (MC) should be sufficient to knit all 3 hats; there will be enough gold from Bumblebee for embellishment for Butterfly.

The 2 vertical bands of MC on the Ladybug and Butterfly hats are worked in intarsia in the round. Load 2 bobbins with MC. When you get to the vertical stripes, bring MC up from under CC and knit; then continue on with same ball of CC.

The spots and markings on the Ladybug and Butterfly Preemie Hats are worked in duplicate stitch after the hat is done.

For smaller (larger) preemie head size, change needle size to change gauge.

Hats

BRIM
With MC, cast on 56 sts and distribute on 4 dpns; place marker for beg of rnd and join, taking care not to twist sts.
Knit 8 rnds.

BODY

Ladybug and Butterfly Hats only
Work appropriate charts and on last rnd, place markers every 7 sts.

Bumblebee Hat only

*Knit 4 rnds CC, knit 4 rnds MC; rep from * once more, then knit 3 rnds CC and on last rnd, place markers every 7 sts.

CROWN

Ladybug and Butterfly Hats only

Dec rnd: *With MC, knit to 2 sts before marker, k2tog; rep from * around—48 sts. Rep Dec rnd until 16 sts rem.

Next rnd: Removing markers, k2tog all around—8 sts.

Bumblebee Hat only

Dec rnd: *With CC, knit to 2 sts before marker, k2tog; rep from * around—48 sts.
   Change to MC and rep Dec rnd until 16 sts rem.

Antenna Stalk

Sl 4 sts to 1 dpn and rem 4 sts to 2nd dpn.
   Work 4-st I-cord on first dpn for 9 rnds/rows.

Antenna Bobble

Rnd 1: Inc1 in each st all around—8 sts.
Rnd 2: Knit.

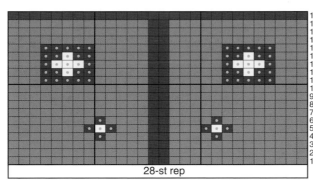

BUTTERFLY CHART

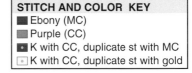

STITCH AND COLOR KEY
- ■ Ebony (MC)
- ■ Purple (CC)
- ▣ K with CC, duplicate st with MC
- ▣ K with CC, duplicate st with gold

STITCH AND COLOR KEY
- ■ Ebony (MC)
- ■ Red (CC)
- ■ K with CC, duplicate st with MC

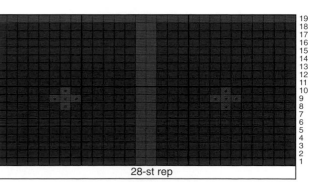

LADYBUG CHART

Rnd 3: Inc1 in each st all around—16 sts.

Rnd 4: K2tog around—8 sts.

Rnd 5: K2tog around—4 sts.

Cut yarn leaving a long tail; Using tapestry needle, thread tail through rem sts, and pull tight. Pass tail through bobble several times so that tail starts to stuff inside of bobble. When bobble is firm enough, pass yarn tail down inside stalk and draw out, cut close to work so tail is hidden inside.

Make another antenna stalk and antenna bobble on rem 4 sts on 2nd dpn.

Close any gaps at top of hat.

Lay both antenna stalks side by side and sew first 3 rnds of one stalk to the other so antennae stand up at base then flop over.

Work duplicate st areas on Ladybug and Butterfly hats.

Weave in all ends. ✪

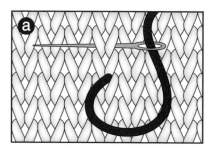

Duplicate Stitch

From underneath piece, bring yarn up in the center of the stitch below the stitch to be duplicated. Place needle from right to left behind both sides of the stitch above the one being duplicated, and pull yarn through (a). Complete the stitch by returning the needle to where you began (b).

Caps for a Cause

When it comes to giving to others in need, what better way than through the loving hands of a knitter? If you're looking to do your part to help newborns in need, here are some highly recommended online resources to get you started:

www.stitchesfromtheheart.org:
Knit and crochet hats, booties, blankets and sweaters for newborn and premature babies.

www.knittingforcharity.org:
Vast resource of charity knitting for babies in need and other knitting charities.

www.yourcause.com:
If you have the desire to start your own charity, this site allows you to create your own Web site and promote the charity of your choice.

The following list offers some of the most comprehensive resources found on the Web:

www.lionbrand.com
www.thedailyknitter.com
www.woolworks.org
www.knitting.about.com

Sassy Swirl Hat

This groovy hat will make those cold-weather blues disappear!

DESIGN BY CELESTE PINHEIRO

 EASY

SIZE
Adult medium

FINISHED MEASUREMENT
Circumference: 21 inches

MATERIALS
- Plymouth Galway Chunky Paint (bulky weight; 100% wool; 123 yds/100g per ball): 1 ball sky blue/lime/mauve #809 (A) **5 BULKY**
- Plymouth Galway Chunky (bulky weight; 100% wool; 123 yds/100g per ball): 1 ball each green #145 (B) and purple #13 (C)
- Size 10½ (6.5mm) double-pointed (set of 5) and 16-inch circular needles or size needed to obtain gauge
- Stitch marker

GAUGE
12 sts and 16 rnds = 4 inches/10cm in St st. To save time, take time to check gauge.

SPECIAL TECHNIQUE
I-Cord: *K4, do not turn, slip sts back to LH needle; rep from * until cord is desired length.

PATTERN NOTE
The hat is worked from top down. Change to circular needle (if desired) when there are enough stitches to do so.

Hat

CROWN
With dpns and A, cast on 8 sts. Distribute evenly on 4 dpns; place marker and join, taking care not to twist sts.
Rnd 1 and all odd-numbered rnds: Knit.
Rnd 2: *K1, yo; rep from * around—16 sts.
Rnd 4: *K2, yo; rep from * around—24 sts.
Rnd 6: *K3, yo; rep from * around—32 sts.
Rnd 8: *K4, yo; rep from * around—40 sts.
Rnd 10: *K5, yo; rep from * around—48 sts.
Rnd 12: *K6, yo; rep from * around—56 sts.
Rnd 14: *K7, yo; rep from * around—64 sts.

BODY
Rnd 1 and all odd-numbered rnds: Knit.
Rnd 2: *Ssk, k6, yo; rep from * around.
Rnd 4: *Yo, ssk, k6; rep from * around.
Rnd 6: *K1, yo, ssk, k5; rep from * around.
Rnd 8: *K2, yo, ssk, k4; rep from * around.
Rnd 10: *K3, yo, ssk, k3; rep from * around.
Rnd 12: *K4, yo, ssk, k2; rep from * around.
Rnd 14: *K5, yo, ssk, k1; rep from * around.

BRIM
Next rnd: Change to B and purl around.
Knit 6 rnds.
Eyelet rnd: *Yo, k2tog, k2; rep from * around.
Knit 9 rnds.
Bind off.

FINISHING
Weave in ends. With B, cast on 4 sts and work I-cord for 28 inches; bind off. Thread through eyelets as in photo. ✿

Funky Chunky Cloche

This fun and chunky hat will make a great impression, while keeping those ears warm!

DESIGN BY ERIKA FLORY

 EASY

SIZE
Woman's small/medium

FINISHED MEASUREMENT
Circumference: 20 inches

MATERIALS
- Colinette Iona (worsted weight; 70% wool/15% kid mohair/15% silk; 160 yds/100g per skein): 1 skein dusk #77
- Size 8 (5mm) double-pointed (set of 4) and 16-inch circular needles or size needed to obtain gauge
- Stitch markers, 1 in CC for beg of rnd

GAUGE
14 sts and 14 rnds = 4 inches/10cm in St st. To save time, take time to check gauge.

PATTERN NOTE
Change to double-pointed needles when stitches no longer fit comfortably on circular needle.

Hat

BODY

With circular needle, cast on 66 sts. Place marker for beg of rnd and join, taking care not twist sts.

*Knit 5 rnds, purl 5 rnds; rep from * once more.

Knit 15 rnds.
Next rnd: *K11, place marker; rep from * around.

CROWN

Dec rnd: *Knit to 2 sts before marker, k2tog; rep from * around—60 sts.
Next 2 rnds: Knit.
  Rep [last 3 rnds] twice more—48 sts.
  Work Dec rnd—42 sts.
  Purl 3 rnds, knit 1 rnd.
  Work Dec rnd—36 sts.
  Knit 1 rnd, purl 3 rnds, knit 1 rnd.
  Work Dec rnd, knit 1 rnd—30 sts.
  Rep [last 2 rnds] 3 times—12 sts.
Next rnd: Removing markers, k2tog around—6 sts.
  Cut yarn, leaving a 5-inch tail.
  Using tapestry needle, thread tail through rem sts, pull tight, then secure tail to WS.

FINISHING

Work in all ends. Block lightly. ✪

Phaidros Grecian Hat

Elegant I-cords draped around a ribbed band evokes the look of ancient Grecian hairstyles.

DESIGN BY JENNIFER TALLAPANENI

 INTERMEDIATE

SIZE

Woman's medium

FINISHED MEASUREMENT

Circumference (slightly stretched): 19 inches

MATERIALS

- Patons Classic Wool Merino (worsted weight; 100% wool; 223 yds/100g per ball): 1 ball each new denim #77115 (MC) and worn denim #77117 (CC)
- Size 5 (3.75mm) 16-inch circular needle
- Size 7 (4.5mm) double-pointed (set of 5) and 16-inch circular needles or size needed to obtain gauge
- Cable needle
- Stitch marker

GAUGE

18 sts and 24 rnds = 4 inches/10cm in St st with larger needles.
To save time, take time to check gauge.

SPECIAL ABBREVIATIONS

3 Over 3 Right Cross (3/3 RC): Sl 3 sts to cn and hold in back, k3, k3 from cn.
3 Over 3 Left Cross (3/3 LC): Sl 3 sts to cn and hold in front, k3, k3 from cn.
Make 1 (M1): Insert LH needle from front to back under the running thread between the last st worked and next st on LH needle. With RH needle, knit into

the back of this loop.

PATTERN STITCHES

Twisted 1x1 Rib (multiple of 2 sts)
Rnd 1: *K1-tbl, p1; rep from * around.
Rnd 2: *K1, p1; rep from * around.
　Rep Rnds 1 and 2 for pat.
Braided Cable (multiple of 14 sts)
Rnds 1, 3, 5, 7: *K11, yo, k2tog, p1; rep from * around.
Rnd 2: *Ssk, yo, k12; rep from * around.
Rnd 4: *Ssk, yo, 3/3 RC, k6; rep from * around.
Rnd 6: *Ssk, yo, k12; rep from * around.
Rnd 8: *Ssk, yo, k3, 3/3 LC, k3; rep from * around.
　Rep Rnds 1–8 for pat.

SPECIAL TECHNIQUE

I-Cord: *K3, do not turn, slip sts back to LH needle; rep from * until cord is desired length. Bind off.

PATTERN NOTES

A chart for the Braided Cable pattern is included for those preferring to work from charts.

　Change to double-pointed needles when stitches no longer fit comfortably on circular needle.

Hat

CUFF

With smaller needle, cast on 84 sts, place marker for beg of rnd and join, being careful not to twist sts.

Work Twisted 1x1 Rib for 1½ inches.
Next rnd: [K1, p1] 5 times, k1, [yo, k2tog] twice, p1, [k1, p1] 32 times, k1, [yo, k2tog] twice, p1, [k1, p1] 5 times.
Next rnd: *K1-tbl, p1; rep from * around.
Rep these 2 rnds twice more.
Continue in Twisted 1x1 Rib until piece measures 3 inches.

BODY

Inc rnd: *K2, M1; rep from * around. (126 sts)
Change to larger circular needle and beg Braided Cable pat.
Work 4 full reps.

CROWN

Rnd 1: *K9, k2tog, yo, k2tog, p1; rep from * around—117 sts.
Rnd 2: *Ssk, yo, k11; rep from * around.
Rnd 3: *K2, ssk, k6, yo, k2tog, p1; rep from * around—108 sts.
Rnd 4: *Ssk, yo, sl 2 sts to cn, hold in back, k3, k2 from cn, k5; rep from * around.
Rnd 5: *K9, yo, k2tog, p1; rep from * around.
Rnd 6: *Ssk, yo, k8, k2tog; rep from * around—99 sts.
Rnd 7: Move marker left 1 st, k1 *k8, yo, p3tog; rep from * around—90 sts.
Rnd 8: *Yo, ssk, k1, sl 3 sts to cn, hold in front, k2, k3 from cn, k2; rep from * around.
Rnd 9: *K8, p2tog; rep from * around—81 sts.
Rnd 10: *Ssk, k7; rep from * around—72 sts.
Rnd 11: *K7, p1; rep from * around.
Rnd 12: *Sl 2 sts to cn, hold in back, k2, k2 from cn, k1, k2tog, k1; rep from * around—63 sts.
Rnd 13: *K6, p1; rep from * around.
Rnd 14: *K4, k2tog, k1; rep from * around—54 sts.
Rnd 15: *Ssk, k3, p1; rep from * around—45 sts.
Rnd 16: *K1, sl 2 sts to cn, hold in front, k1, k2 from cn, k1; rep from * around.
Rnd 17: *Ssk, k2, p1; rep from * around—36 sts.
Rnd 18: *Ssk, k2; rep from * around—27 sts.
Rnd 19: *Ssk, p1; rep from * around—18 sts.
Rnd 20: *Ssk; rep from * around—9 sts.
Cut yarn, leaving a 5-inch tail.
Using tapestry needle, thread tail through rem sts, and pull tight. Secure on WS.

FINISHING

Weave in all ends. Block lightly.

I-CORD

With CC and smaller needle, cast on 3 sts. Work I-cord for 63 inches or long enough to wrap around your head 3 times. Weave I-cord through yo's on sides of cuff, wrapping around 3 times and ending with tails in center back. Tie or sew I-cord ends tog. ✪

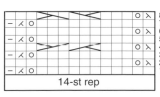

BRAIDED CABLE

STITCH KEY
☐ Knit
⊙ Yo
⋌ K2tog
− Purl
⋋ Ssk
3/3 RC
3/3 LC

Corkscrew Tam

This playful two-toned tam creates a little pizzazz, and puts a new spin on a traditional shape.

DESIGN BY ERIKA FLORY

◧◧▢▷ EASY

SIZE
Woman's small/medium

FINISHED MEASUREMENT
Circumference: 20 inches

MATERIALS
- Plymouth Galway (worsted weight; 100% wool; 210 yds/100g per ball): 1 ball each plum #92 (MC) and cocoa #144 (CC)
- Size 6 (4mm) 16-inch circular needle
- Size 8 (5mm) double-pointed (set of 5) and 16-inch circular needles or size needed to obtain gauge
- Stitch markers, 1 in CC for beg of rnd

GAUGE
16 sts and 20 rnds = 4 inches/10cm in St st with larger needles.
To save time, take time to check gauge.

SPECIAL ABBREVIATIONS
Make 1 (M1): Insert LH needle from front to back under the running thread between the last st worked and next st on LH needle. With RH needle, knit into the back of this loop.

Increase 2 sts (Inc2): Knit in front loop, then in back loop, then in front loop of same st.

PATTERN NOTE
Change to double-pointed needles when stitches no longer fit comfortably on circular needle.

Hat

BRIM

With smaller needle and CC, cast on 76 sts; place marker for beg of rnd and join, being careful not to twist sts.

Knit 2 rnds.

Next 5 rnds: *K1 CC, p1 MC; rep from * around.

Cut CC.

CROWN

Rnd 1: With larger needle and MC, knit around.

Rnd 2 (inc): *K2, M1; rep from * around—114 sts.

Work even in St st until piece measures 4¾ inches from beg.

Next rnd: *K19, place marker; rep from * around.

Dec rnd: *Knit to 2 sts before marker, k2tog; rep from * around—108 sts.

Rep [Dec rnd] 17 times—6 sts.

Cut yarn leaving a 6-inch tail.

Using tapestry needle, thread tail through rem sts, and pull tight.

CORKSCREW TASSELS

Make 3

With smaller needle and CC, cast on 25 sts.

Knit 1 row.

Next row: Inc2 in each st across—75 sts.

Bind off.

FINISHING

Sew corkscrew tassels firmly to top of hat. Weave in all ends. Block. ✪

Arctic Ear Flap Cap

Keep those ears warm and toasty wearing the coolest cap on the block!

DESIGN BY ELLEN EDWARDS DRECHSLER

◀▮▮◻◻ EASY

SIZE
Adult medium

FINISHED MEASUREMENT
Circumference: 21 inches

MATERIALS
- Colinette Iona (worsted weight; 70% wool/15% kid mohair/15% silk; 154 yds/100g per skein): 1 skein copperbeech #67
- Size 6 (4mm) 16-inch circular needle
- Size 8 (5mm) double-pointed and 16-inch circular needles or size needed to obtain gauge
- Stitch holder
- Stitch markers, 1 in CC for beg of rnd

GAUGE

16 sts and 24 rnds = 4 inches/10cm in St st with larger needle.
To save time, take time to check gauge.

SPECIAL TECHNIQUE

I-Cord: *K5, do not turn, slip sts back to LH needle; rep from * until cord is desired length.

PATTERN NOTE

Change to double-pointed needles when stitches no longer fit comfortably on circular needle.

Hat

BODY

With larger circular needle, cast on 84 sts; place marker for beg of rnd and join, taking care not to twist sts.

Knit every rnd until piece measures approx 6 inches from beg.
Next rnd: K12, place marker; rep from * around.

CROWN

Dec rnd: *Knit to 2 sts from marker, k2tog; rep from * around—77 sts.

Rep Dec rnd [every other rnd] 9 times—14 sts.

Next rnd: Removing markers, K2tog around—7 sts.

Cut yarn, leaving a 5-inch tail.

Using tapestry needle, thread tail through rem sts, pull tight and secure to WS.

Weave in all ends.

EAR FLAPS

With smaller circular needle, pick up and knit 86 sts around cast on edge of hat; place marker for beg of rnd and join.

Purl 1 rnd, knit 1 rnd, purl 1 rnd.

Next rnd: K15, bind off 28 sts, k15 and slip sts to holder, bind off 28 sts—15 sts rem on needle.

**Knit 12 rows.

Dec row: Ssk, knit to end of row.

Rep Dec row every row until 5 sts rem.

Work I-cord for 14 inches or desired length.

Bind off.

Slip sts from holder to needle and reattach yarn.

Work 2nd flap as for first, beg at **.

FINISHING

Weave in ends. Tie a knot in the end of each I-cord. ✪

Lacy Chain-Link Cable Head & Neck Warmer

Choose your mood—wear this versatile warmer as a hat or to simply keep your neck fashionably warm.

DESIGN BY CELESTE PINHEIRO

 EASY

SIZE
Adult average

FINISHED MEASUREMENTS
Circumference (laced up): 20 inches
Width: 6½ inches

MATERIALS
- Classic Elite Yarns Inca Alpaca (worsted weight; 100% alpaca; 109 yds/50g per hank): 2 hanks Kentucky teal #1120
- Size 4 (3.5mm) needles
- Size 6 (4mm) needles or size needed to obtain gauge

GAUGE
37 sts and 30 rows = 4 inches/10cm in lace pat (unstretched) with larger needles.
To save time take time to check gauge.

PATTERN STITCH
Lace Pat (multiple of 5 sts + 7)
Rows 1, 3, and 5 (WS): K2, *p3, k2; rep from * to end.
Row 2 (RS): K2, *yo, sk2p, yo, p2; rep from * to last 5 sts, yo, sk2p, yo, k2.
Row 4: K2, *k1, yo, ssk, p2; rep from * to last 5 sts, k1, yo, ssk, k2.
Row 6: K2, *k3, p2; rep from * to last 5 sts, k5.
   Rep Rows 1–6 for pat.

SPECIAL TECHNIQUE
I-Cord: *K4, do not turn, slip sts back to LH needle; rep from * until cord is desired length. Bind off.

PATTERN NOTES

This piece is worked flat from end-to-end; the 2 ends are joined into a circle by lacing I-cords through the eyelets at the edges.

A chart for the Lace pattern is included for those preferring to work from charts.

HEADBAND

With smaller needles, cast on 43 sts.

Row 1 (WS): Knit.

Row 2 (Eyelet row): *K2tog, yo; rep from * to last 3 sts, k3.

Row 3: Knit across and dec 1 st—42 sts.

Rows 4-6: Knit.

Next row: Change to larger needles and beg Lace pat.

Work even until piece measures 19 inches, ending on Row 5 of Lace pat.

Change to smaller needles, and knit 4 rows, and on last row, inc 1 st—43 sts.

Next row: Rep Eyelet row.

Next row: Knit.
Bind off.

FINISHING

Weave in all ends. Block as necessary.

I-CORD TIE

With larger needles, cast on 4 sts. Work I-cord for approx 36 inches. Bind off. Thread through eyelets as in photo and tie in bow. Knot ends of tie. ✪

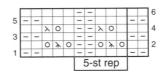

LACE PATTERN

STITCH KEY	
⊟	P on RS, k on WS
☐	K on RS, p on WS
⊙	Yo
⅄	Sk2p
⅃	Ssk

Three-Toned Topper

Try your hand at some simple color knitting with this three-toned Fair Isle-patterned cap.

DESIGN BY ERSSIE MAJOR

◖◼◼◻ INTERMEDIATE

SIZE
Woman's average

FINISHED MEASUREMENTS
Circumference: 19 inches
Height: 8 inches

MATERIALS
- Debbie Bliss Cashmerino Aran (worsted weight; 55% merino/33% microfiber/12% cashmere; 98 yds/50g per ball): 1 ball each dark purple #14 (A), med purple #17 (B) and light purple #19 (C)
- Size 7 (4.5mm) 16-inch circular needle
- Size 8 (5mm) double-pointed (set of 5) and 16-inch circular needles or size needed to obtain gauge
- Stitch markers

GAUGE
18 sts and 24 rnds = 4 inches/10cm in Fair Isle pat with larger needles.
To save time, take time to check gauge.

PATTERN NOTE
Change to double-pointed needles when stitches no longer fit comfortably on circular needle.

Hat

CUFF
With smaller circular needle and A, cast on 96 sts; place marker for beg of rnd and join, taking care not to twist sts.
Work 8 rnds in K2, P2 Rib.

BODY
Change to larger needle, work Rnds 1–18 of Fair Isle Chart, then work Rnds 1–8 once more, placing markers every 24 sts on last rnd.

CROWN

Dec rnd: Continuing in established pattern, k2tog, work to last 2 sts, ssk—88 sts.

Rep Dec rnd every rnd until 8 sts rem, removing markers on last rnd.

Cut yarn, leaving a 5-inch tail.

Using tapestry needle, thread tail through rem sts, pull tight and secure on WS.

FINISHING

Weave in all ends. Hand wash and block to finished measurements. ✪

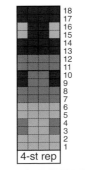

COLOR KEY
■ A
■ B
□ C

FAIR ISLE CHART

4-st rep

Bobble Lace Beanie

If you're in the mood for bunches of bobbles, this light-weight lacy skullcap makes for a special project.

DESIGN BY CELESTE PINHEIRO

 INTERMEDIATE

SIZE
Woman's average

FINISHED MEASUREMENT
Circumference: 20 inches (unstretched)

MATERIALS
- Classic Elite Yarns Wool Bam Boo (DK weight; 50% wool/50% bamboo; 118 yds/50g per ball): 2 balls vanilla #1650
- Size 6 (4mm) double-pointed and 16-inch circular needles or size needed to obtain gauge

GAUGE
32 sts and 40 rnds= 5 inches/12.7cm in Bobble Lace pat (unstretched).
To save time take time to check gauge.

SPECIAL ABBREVIATION
Make bobble (MB): [K1, p1, k1, p1, k1] into st, pass first 4 sts over 5th st.

PATTERN STITCH
Bobble Lace (multiple of 16 sts)
Rnd 1: *P2, k1, MB, k3, MB, k1, p2, k5; rep from * around.
Rnd 2: *P2, k2, p3, k2, p2, k5; rep from * around.
Rnd 3: *P2, k7, p2, k2tog, yo, k1, yo, ssk; rep from * around.

Rnd 4: Rep Rnd 2.
Rep Rnds 1–4 for pat.

PATTERN NOTES
A chart for the Bobble Lace pat is included for those preferring to work from charts.

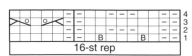

BOBBLE LACE

16-st rep

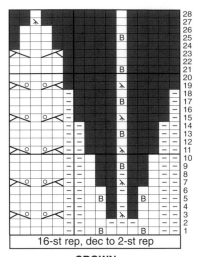

16-st rep, dec to 2-st rep

CROWN

STITCH KEY

—	P
	K
B	MB
	K2tog, yo
	Yo, ssk
	Sk2p
■	No stitch
	K2tog
	Ssk

Change to double-pointed needles when stitches no longer fit comfortably on circular needle.

Hat

BODY

Cast on 128 sts; place marker for beg of rnd and join, taking care not to twist sts.

Work 5 rnds in P2, K2 Rib.

Work 28 rnds (7 reps) of Bobble Lace pat.

CROWN

Dec for crown, following chart—8 sts.

FINISHING

Cut yarn, leaving a 5-inch tail. Using tapestry needle, thread tail through rem sts, and pull tight; secure on WS. Weave in all ends. Block as necessary. ✪

Nordic Tasseled Tam
Stay fashionably warm in this wintry creation.

DESIGN BY CELESTE PINHEIRO

 INTERMEDIATE

SIZE
Adult medium

FINISHED MEASUREMENT
Circumference: 21 inches

MATERIALS
• Nashua Handknits Creative Focus Worsted (worsted weight; 75% wool/25% alpaca; 220 yds/50g per ball): 1 ball each espresso #0410 (A), natural #0100 (B)
• Size 8 (5mm) double-pointed and 16-inch circular needles or size needed to obtain gauge
• Stitch marker

4 MEDIUM

GAUGE

20 sts and 20 rnds = 4 inches/10cm in stranded St st.
To save time, take time to check gauge.

PATTERN STITCHES

Braid (multiple of 2 sts)
Rnd 1: *K1 A, k1 B; rep from * around.
Rnd 2: Carrying both yarns on RS and bringing one strand over the previous strand when working it, *p1 A, p1 B; rep from * around.
Rnd 3: Carrying both yarns on RS and bringing one strand under the previous strand when working it, *p1 A, p1 B; rep from * around.

FAIR ISLE PATTERN

See Fair Isle chart on page 56.

PATTERN NOTE

When working the Braid, the yarns will spiral around each other on Round 2; do not untwist them because they will untwist themselves on Round 3.

Hat

BODY

With circular needle and A, cast on 98 sts; place marker for beg of rnd and join, taking care not to twist sts.
Knit 1 rnd, purl 1 rnd, knit 1 rnd.
Next 3 rnds: Work Braid pat.
With A, *knit 1 rnd, purl 1 rnd; rep from * once.
Following chart, work 1 rep of Fair Isle pat.

CROWN

Rnd 1: With A, knit and dec 3 sts evenly around—95 sts.
Rnd 2: Purl.
Rnd 3: Work Crown chart 5 times around—85 sts.
Complete Crown chart—5 sts rem.
Cut yarn, leaving a 5-inch tail.
Using tapestry needle, thread tail through rem sts, and pull tight.

FINISHING

Weave in all ends.
Cut 6 strands of each color, each approx 15 inches long. Hold strands tog and tie an overhand knot in the middle. Make braids on either side of knot, then knot ends. Attach to top of hat. ✪

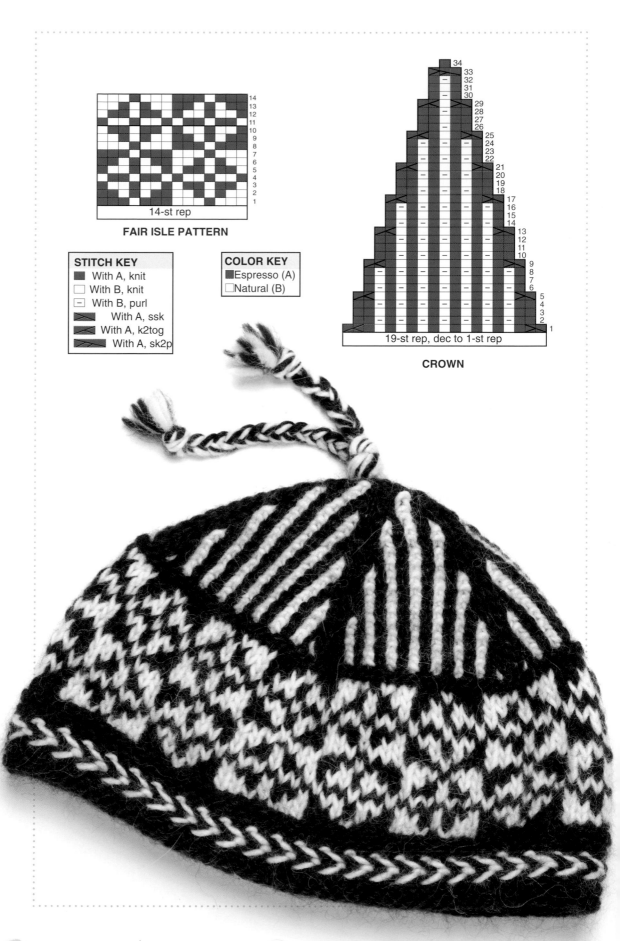

FAIR ISLE PATTERN

14-st rep

STITCH KEY
- ■ With A, knit
- □ With B, knit
- ⊟ With B, purl
- With A, ssk
- With A, k2tog
- With A, sk2p

COLOR KEY
- ■ Espresso (A)
- □ Natural (B)

CROWN

19-st rep, dec to 1-st rep

Plush Stripes Hat

Contrasting matte and shiny stripes make this hat a stunning addition to any wardrobe.

DESIGN BY DIANE ZANGL

 **INTERMEDIATE**

SIZE
Woman's average

FINISHED MEASUREMENTS
Circumference: 20 inches
Height (with crown folded down): 8 inches

MATERIALS
- Plymouth Baby Alpaca Grande (bulky weight; 100% baby alpaca; 110 yds/100g per skein): 2 skeins cherry red #2050 (MC)
- Plymouth Sinsation (bulky weight; 80% rayon/20% wool; 38 yds/50g per ball): 2 balls cherry red #3375 (CC)
- Size 9 (5.5mm) straight and 16-inch circular needles or size needed to obtain gauge
- Stitch markers
- Stitch holder

5 BULKY

GAUGE
16 sts and 20 rows = 4 inches/10cm in St st with MC.
To save time, take time to check gauge.

SPECIAL ABBREVIATION
Wrap and Turn (W&T): Bring yarn to RS of work between needles, slip next st pwise to RH needle, bring yarn around this st to WS, slip st back to LH needle, turn work to begin working back in the other direction.

SPECIAL TECHNIQUES
Hiding wraps: Pick up wrap from front to back and knit tog with wrapped st.
I-Cord: *K3, do not turn, slip sts back to LH needle; rep from * until cord is desired length.

The body and crown of this hat are worked lengthwise using short rows.

For a shorter hat, cast on 4 stitches fewer for every inch shorter that you would like it; follow rest of pattern as written.

Hat

BODY

With MC, cast on 36 sts.
Row 1 (WS): Purl.
Row 2: Knit to last 4 sts, W&T.
Row 3: Purl.
Row 4: Knit to last 8 sts, W&T.
Row 5: Purl.
Row 6: Change to CC. Knit all sts, hiding wraps as you come to them.
Row 7: Knit.
Row 8: Purl to last 4 sts, W&T
Row 9: Knit.
Row 10: Purl to last 8 sts, W&T.
Row 11: Knit.
Row 12: Change to MC and rep Row 6.
Rep [Rows 1–12] 8 times more.
Bind off.
Sew bound off and cast on edges tog. Gather top (shaped) edge and sew tog tightly.

CUFF

With RS facing and using circular needle and MC, beg at seam, pick up and knit 5 sts in each section along lower edge; place marker for beg of rnd—90 sts.

Work 5 rnds in K1, P1 Rib, ending last rnd 5 sts before marker.

EAR FLAPS AND TIES

Next rnd: Bind off 33 sts, work established rib over next 11 sts and place on holder, bind off 35, work established rib over rem 11 sts. Work in rows from this point.
**Row 1 (WS): Sl 1 pwise wyif, knit to end of row.

Rep [Row 1] 8 times more.
Dec row: Sl 1 pwise wyif, k2tog, knit to end of row.
Rep Dec row until 3 sts rem.
Work I-Cord for 5 inches, then k3tog and fasten off last st.
For 2nd flap, slip sts from holder to needle.
With WS facing, join MC and work as for first flap from ** to end.

LOOP TASSEL

With MC, pick up and knit 3 sts at top of hat.
Work I-Cord for 10 inches, then k3tog and fasten off last st.
Cut yarn, leaving a 10-inch tail.

FINISHING

Sew end of cord to top of hat. Fold cord into 3 loops, and sew to top with rem yarn tail (see photo). Weave in ends. Block lightly. ✪

Twisted Rib Cap

This attractive cap features a classic look that appeals to men, women and children alike.

DESIGN BY FAINA GOBERSTEIN

■■□□ EASY

SIZES

Child (adult) Instructions are given for smaller size, with larger size in parentheses. When only 1 number is given, it applies to both sizes.

FINISHED MEASUREMENT

Circumference: 18 (21) inches

MATERIALS

- Brown Sheep Top of the Lamb Worsted (worsted weight; 100% wool; 190 yds/4 oz per skein): 1 skein terra cotta #235
- Size 8 (5mm) 16-inch circular needle
- Size 10 (6mm) double-pointed (set of 5) and 16-inch circular needles or size needed to obtain gauge
- Stitch marker

GAUGE

20 sts and 24 rows = 4 inches/10cm in Twisted Cable Rib.
To save time, take time to check gauge.

SPECIAL ABBREVIATIONS

Left Twist (LT): Skip first st, knit 2nd st tbl; do not slip st from LH needle. Knit skipped st in front loop. Slip both sts off needle at the same time.

Left Twist Decrease (LTDec): Skip first st, k2tog-tbl; do not slip st from LH needle. Knit skipped st into front loop. Slip both sts off needle at the same time.

PATTERN STITCHES

Twisted 1x1 Rib (multiple of 2 sts)
Rnd 1: *K1-tbl, p1; rep from * around.
  Rep Rnd 1 for pat.
Twisted Cable Rib (multiple of 4 sts)
Rnd 1: *LT, p2; rep from * around.
Rnd 2: *K2, p2; rep from * around.
  Rep Rnds 1 and 2 for pat.

PATTERN NOTE

Change to double-pointed needles when stitches no longer fit comfortably on circular needle.

Hat

BAND

With smaller needle, cast on 88 (104) sts. Place marker for beg of rnd and join, being careful not to twist sts.
  Work in Twisted 1x1 Rib for 1 inch.

BODY

Change to larger needle and work in Twisted Cable Rib until piece measures 5 (6½) inches from beg, ending with Rnd 2.

CROWN

Rnd 1: *LT, p2tog; rep from * around—66 (78) sts.
Rnd 2: *K2, p1; rep from * around.
Rnd 3: *LT, p1; rep from * around.
Rnd 4: *K1, k2tog-tbl; rep from * around—44 (52) sts
Rnd 5: K1, *LTDec; rep from * to last 1 (0) sts, k1 (0)—30 (35) sts.
Rnd 6: Knit.

Rnd 7: *LTDec; rep from * to last 0 (2) sts, k0 (2)—20 (24) sts.
Rnd 8: K2tog-tbl around—10 (12) sts. Cut yarn, leaving a 6-inch tail.
  With tapestry needle, pull yarn through rem sts; fasten securely on WS.

FINISHING

Weave in all ends. Block lightly. ✿

Segmented Scandinavian Cloche

Create an elegant and timeless look with this richly-patterned cloche.

DESIGN BY LOIS YOUNG

▰▰▰▱ INTERMEDIATE

SIZE
Adult Medium

FINISHED MEASUREMENTS
Circumference: 22 inches (excluding brim)
Height: 9 inches (including brim)

MATERIALS
- Brown Sheep Company Nature Spun Sport (sport weight; 100% wool; 184 yds/50g per skein): 1 skein each pomegranate #146 (MC) and pepper #601 (CC)
- Size 3 (3.25 mm) double-pointed and 24-inch circular needles or size needed to obtain gauge
- Stitch markers, 1 in CC for beg of rnd

2 FINE

GAUGE

29-st pat rep = 4½ inches/10.5 cm; 26 rnds = 4 inches/10cm in stranded St st. To save time, take time to check gauge.

PATTERN STITCH

Color pat: See chart.

PATTERN NOTES

Hat is worked from the pattern bands to the top; the brim is picked up and knit down from the cast on edge.

Change to double-pointed needles when stitches no longer fit comfortably on circular needle.

Hat

BODY AND CROWN

With circular needle and MC, cast on 145 sts; place marker for beg of rnd and join, taking care not to twist sts.
Rnd 1: Purl.
Rnd 2: Knit.
Rnd 3: *P29, place marker; rep from * around.
Work Rnds 1–44 of Chart—5 sts rem.
Cut yarn, leaving 4-inch tail.
Using tapestry needle, thread tail through rem sts, pull tight and secure to WS.

BRIM

With circular needle and CC, pick up and knit 144 sts around bottom of hat.
Rnd 1: *Purl and knit in next st, k11, rep from * around—156 sts.
Rnd 2: Knit.
Rnd 3: *K3 CC, k3 MC, rep from * around.
Rnd 4: *K3 MC, k3 CC, rep from * around.
Rnd 5: Knit with CC.
Rnd 6: Purl with CC.
Rnd 7: Knit with MC.
Rnd 8: Purl with MC.
Rnds 9 and 10: Rep Rnds 7 and 8.

Rnds 11–20: Knit with CC.

Bind-off rnd: *K11, k2tog, binding off as you go; rep from * around.

FINISHING

Turn hem to inside of brim along MC garter st band; whipstitch hem to cast on edge of hat. Weave in ends. Block lightly. ✿

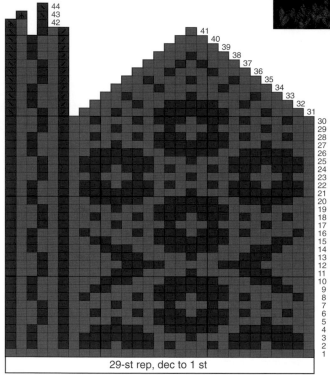

29-st rep, dec to 1 st

SEGMENTED SCANDINAVIAN CLOCHE

STITCH AND COLOR KEY	
■	Knit with CC
■	Knit with MC
◪	K2tog with MC
◩	Ssk with MC
▨	[Sl 1, k2tog, psso] with MC
▧	[Sl 2 tog kwise, psso] with MC

Twisted Basket Weave Newsboy

Look ultra cool and fabulously "fashion-forward" in this chunky cap.

DESIGN BY KARA GOTT WARNER

◼◼◼◻ INTERMEDIATE

SIZE
Adult average

FINISHED MEASUREMENT
Circumference: 21 inches

MATERIALS
- Schaefer Yarn Esperanza (bulky weight; 70% lambswool/30% alpaca; 280 yds/8 oz per skein): 1 skein Dian Fossey
- Size 10 (6mm) 16-inch circular needle or size needed to obtain gauge
- Size H/8 (5mm) crochet hook
- 1 stitch marker

5 BULKY

GAUGE
14 sts and 20 rows= 4 inches/10cm in St st.
To save time, take time to check gauge.

SPECIAL ABBREVIATIONS
Wrap and Turn (W&T): Bring yarn to RS of work between needles, slip next st pwise to RH needle, bring yarn around this st to WS, slip st back to LH needle, turn work to begin working back in the other direction.

Work wrapped sts and wraps tog (WW): *On RS:* Knit to wrapped st, slip the wrapped st pwise from LH needle to RH needle. Use tip of LH needle to pick up wrap(s) and place it/them on RH needle. Slip wrap(s) and st back to LH needle and knit them tog.

On WS: Purl to wrapped st, slip the wrapped st kwise from LH needle to RH needle. Use tip of LH to pick up wrap(s) and place it/them on RH needle. Slip wrap(s) and st back to LH needle and purl them tog.

PATTERN STITCH

Twisted Basket Weave (even number of sts)
Rnd 1: Skip the first st, k1-tbl in 2nd st, then knit the first st through the front loop; slip both sts off the LH needle.
Rnd 2: Knit.
Rep Rnds 1 and 2 for pat.

SPECIAL TECHNIQUE

Provisional Cast-On: With crochet hook and waste yarn, make a chain several sts longer than desired cast on. With knitting needle and project yarn, pick up indicated number of sts in the "bumps" on back of chain. When indicated in pattern, "unzip" the crochet chain to free live sts.

PATTERN NOTES

Hat is worked from the top down. Crown and visor are worked back and forth using short rows.

Stitches are picked up around the

crown and the body is worked in the round. The visor is worked separately and sewn on.

Hat

Cast on 12 sts.
Row 1 (WS): Purl.
Row 2 (RS): K3, W&T.
Row 3: P3.
Row 4: K3, WW, k2, W&T.
Row 5: P6.
Row 6: K6, WW, k2, W&T.
Row 7: P9.
Row 8: K9, W&T. (St is double-wrapped.)
Row 9: P9.
Row 10: K6, W&T.
Row 11: P6.
Row 12: K3, W&T.
Row 13: P3.
Row 14: K1, W&T.

Row 15: P1.
Row 16: Knit across all sts, working all wraps tog with sts (4 wrapped sts total).
   Rep [Rows 1–16] 5 times more.
   Purl 1 row.
   Bind off all sts.
   Block.
   Sew the bound off edge to the cast on edge to form a circle.
   With crochet hook, pick up sts inside opening at center top and work 2 rnds of sc to close gap. Fasten off.

BODY

With RS facing, pick up and knit 92 sts along outside edge of crown; place marker for beg of rnd.
   Work in Twisted Basket Weave pat for 3 inches.

BAND

Rnd 1: Purl.
Rnd 2: K2, [k2tog, k8, k2tog, k4] 5 times, k2tog, k8—81 sts.

Rnds 3 and 4: Knit.
Rnd 5: K11, [k2tog, k15] 4 times, k2tog—76 sts.
Rnd 6: Knit.
  Bind off.

Using provisional method, cast on 28 sts.
Row 1: Purl.
Row 2: Knit to last 2 sts, W&T.
Row 3: Purl to last 2 sts, W&T.
Row 4: Knit to 1 st before last wrapped st, W&T.
Row 5: Purl to 1 st before last wrapped st, W&T.
  Rep Rows 4 and 5 until 12 sts rem unwrapped in center.
Row 6: Knit to wrapped st, WW, W&T.
Row 7: Purl to wrapped st, WW, W&T.
  Rep Rows 6 and 7 until 1 wrapped st rem at each end.
Row 8: Knit to wrapped st, WW, k1.
Row 9: Purl to wrapped st, WW, p1.

Row 1 (RS): K4, W&T.
Row 2: P4.
Row 3: K3, W&T.

Row 4: P3.
Row 5: K2, W&T.
Row 6: P2.
Row 7: K1, W&T.
Row 8: P1.
Row 9: Knit across row, working all wraps tog with sts.
Row 10: P4, W&T.
Row 11: K4.
Row 12: P3, W&T.
Row 13: K3.
Row 14: P2, W&T.
Row 15: K2.
Row 16: P1, W&T.
Row 17: K1.
Row 18: Purl across row, working all wraps tog with sts.
  Bind off loosely.
  Remove waste yarn from cast on row and slip 28 live sts to needle.
  Rep Rows 1–18 of visor shaping.

Sew edge of brim closed where short rows were just created. Sew brim to edge of hat, easing as you go. Weave in ends, block lightly. ✪

Tiger-Striped Toque

Hit the streets in style wearing this two-toned striped cap.

DESIGN BY LAURA ANDERSSON

 EASY

SIZE
Fits most adults and teens

FINISHED MEASUREMENT
Circumference: 21 inches

MATERIALS
- Crystal Palace Yarns Aran yarn (worsted weight; 100% wool; 102 yds/50g per ball): 1 ball each redwood #1014 (A) and yellow gold #1004 (B)
- Size 9 (5.5mm) double-pointed (set of 4) and 16-inch circular needles or size needed to obtain gauge

GAUGE
16 sts and 20 rnds = 4 inches/10cm in St st.
To save time, take time to check gauge.

SPECIAL ABBREVIATIONS
N1, N2: Needle 1, Needle 2
Make 1 (M1): Insert LH needle from front to back under the running thread between the last st worked and next st on LH needle. With RH needle, knit into back of this loop.

PATTERN STITCHES
Corrugated Rib A (multiple of 4 sts)
Rnd 1: *K2 A, p2 B; rep from * around.

Rep Rnd 1 for pat.
Corrugated Rib B (multiple of 4 sts)
Rnd 1: *K2 B, p2 A; rep from * around.
Rep Rnd 1 for pat.

SPECIAL TECHNIQUE
I-Cord: *K4, do not turn, slip sts back to LH needle; rep from * until cord is desired length.

PATTERN NOTES
Do not cut yarn not in use; twist A & B at beg of every round.

When decreasing crown, change to double-pointed needles when stitches no longer fit comfortably on circular needle.

Hat

TIE
With dpn and A, cast on 4 sts.
Work I-cord for 18 inches (or desired length).

EARFLAPS
Row 1 (WS): K1, p2, k1.
Row 2: K1, M1, p2, M1, k2—6 sts.
Rows 3, 5, 7, 9, 11, 13: K1, purl to last st, k1.
Row 4: K1, M1, k2, p2, k2, M1, k1—8 sts.
Row 6: K1, M1, k3, p2, k3, M1, k1—10 sts.
Row 8: K1, M1, k4, p2, k4, M1, k1—12 sts.
Row 10: K1, M1, k5, p2, k5, M1, k1—14 sts.
Row 12: K1, M1, k6, p2, k6, M1, k1—16 sts.

Row 14: K1, M1, k7, p2, k7, M1, k1—18 sts.

Row 15: K1, purl to last st, k1.

Row 16 (RS): K8, p2, k8.

Rep Rows 15 and 16 until Earflap measures 3½ inches from I-cord ties and ending with Row 15.

Cut yarn, leaving an 8-inch tail and leave sts on dpn.

Work 2nd tie and Earflap to match first. Do not cut yarn.

Rnd 1: With circular needle, work Row 16 across 2nd earflap sts; turn work and using cable method, cast on 24 sts; turn work again and with RS facing, work Row 16 across first earflap sts; turn work and using cable method, cast on 24 sts; turn work so that RS is facing again; place marker for beg of rnd and join, taking care not to twist sts—84 sts.

With A, purl 3 rnds, knit 3 rnds.

Join B and knit 2 rnds.

With A, knit 2 rnds.

Work 8 rnds Corrugated Rib B.

With B, knit 3 rnds.

With A, knit 2 rnds.

With B, knit 2 rnds.

Work 8 rnds Corrugated Rib A.

With A, knit 3 rnds.

With B, knit 1 rnd.

Rnd 1 (dec): *K2tog B, [k1 B, k1 A] 5 times; rep from * around—77 sts.

Rnd 2 and all even-numbered rnds: Knit the colors as they present themselves.

Rnd 3 (dec): *K2tog B, [k1 B, k1 A] 4 times, k1 B; rep from * around—70 sts.

Rnd 5 (dec): *K2tog B, [k1 B, k1 A] 4 times; rep from * around—63 sts.

Rnd 7 (dec): *K2tog B, [k1 B, k1 A] 3 times, k1 B; rep from * around—56 sts.

Rnd 9 (dec): *K2tog B, [k1 B, k1 A] 3 times; rep from * around—49 sts.

Rnd 11 (dec): *K2tog B, [k1 B, k1 A] twice, k1 B; rep from * around—42 sts.

Rnd 13 (dec): *K2tog B, [k1 B, k1 A] twice; rep from * around—35 sts.

Rnd 15 (dec): *K2tog B, k1 B, k1 A, k1 B; rep from * around—28 sts.

Rnd 17 (dec): *K2tog B, k1 B, k1 A; rep from * around—21 sts.

Rnd 19 (dec): *K2tog B, k1 A; rep from * around—14 sts.

Rnd 20: Rep Rnd 2.

  *K2tog B, k2tog A; rep from * until 4 sts rem.

FINISHING

Option 1: Bind off, alternating k1 A, k1 B.

Option 2: Work checked I-cord of desired length, alternating k1A, k1B and working each new st with the opposite color of st on needle, then bind off and cut yarns, leaving an 8-inch tail. With tapestry needle, pull yarns down into I-cord about 3–4 inches, then cut ends, hiding them inside.

  Weave in all ends. Block as necessary. ✪

We all have stories about why we love to make socks. We wear them, share them and maybe even trade with others. We may knit them for endless hours amongst a circle of friends or alone during a day in the park. They are perfectly compact, making them great companions when we're out and about. Take your pick from the abundance of projects ahead. Pack those totes and head out for some new adventures!

TOES

Anatomy of a Sock

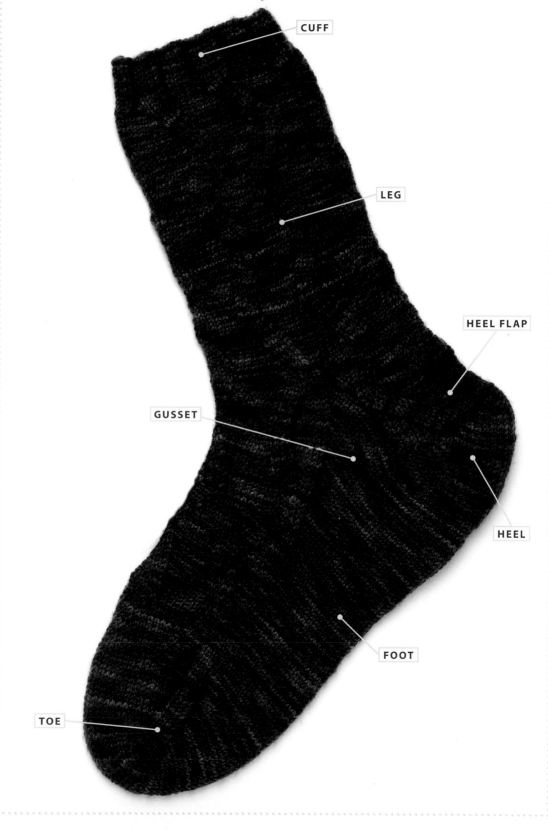

CUFF

LEG

HEEL FLAP

GUSSET

HEEL

FOOT

TOE

Playful Polka Dot Socks

We aren't all brave enough to wear yellow polka dot bikinis, but why not some polka dot socks?

DESIGN BY JOANNE SEIFF

SIZES
Child's small (child's large, woman's small, woman's large) to fit child's shoe sizes 9–12 (child's 13–3, woman's 5–7, woman's 8–10) Instructions are given for smallest size, with larger sizes in parentheses. When only 1 number is given, it applies to all sizes.

FINISHED MEASUREMENTS
Circumference: 6 (7, 8, 9) inches
Foot length: 7 (8, 9, 10) inches

MATERIALS
- Knit Picks Palette (fingering weight; 100% wool; 231 yds/50g per ball): 1 ball each black #23729 (A), hyacinth #23721 (B) and petal #23717 (C)
- Size 1 (2.25mm) double-pointed needles (set of 4) or size needed to obtain gauge
- Stitch marker

GAUGE
32 sts and 38 rows = 4 inches in stranded St st.
To save time, take time to check gauge.

SPECIAL ABBREVIATIONS
N1, N2, N3: Needle 1, Needle 2, Needle 3
Backwards Yarnover (B-yo): With WS facing, bring yarn to the back under needle, and then over the top; the leading side of the loop will be on the back of the needle.

PATTERN NOTES
This sock is worked on 3 double-pointed needles from the cuff down with short-row heel and toe.

Work 2 gauge swatches and if necessary, go up in needle size for stranded stockinette stitch section.

The color work is stranded Fair-Isle style; weave in stranded color every 3 stitches to avoid long floats. Carry 3rd color not-in-use up the back, twisting it around other 2 colors every other round.

Socks

CUFF
With A, loosely cast on 48 (56, 64, 72) sts and distribute sts as follows: N1: 12 (14, 16, 18) sts; N2: 24 (28, 32, 36) sts; N3: 12 (14, 16, 18) sts. Place marker for beg of rnd and join, taking care not to twist sts. Work K2, P2 Rib for 1 inch.

Join B.

Work 1 (2, 2, 3) reps of chart or until cuff measures desired length, ending with Rnd 10.

With A, knit 1 rnd.

Cut A and B, leaving 4-inch tails.

HEEL

Note: *Heel is worked on N1 and N3 only.*

**Row 1 (RS): On N1, k11 (13, 15, 17), turn.

Row 2: On N1 and continuing to N3, B-yo, p22 (26, 30, 34), turn.

Row 3: Yo, k21 (25, 29, 33), turn.

Row 4: B-yo, purl to first set of paired sts (st with yo attached), turn.

Row 5: Yo, knit to first set of paired sts, turn.

Rep Rows 4 and 5, working 1 fewer st before turning on each succeeding row, until 8 (10, 12, 14) sts rem between the yo's, ending with Row 4.

Next row (RS): Yo, k8 (10, 12, 14), k2tog-tbl (the yo and next st on needle, closing the gap), turn.

Next row: B-yo, p9 (11, 13, 15), p2tog (the yo and next st on needle, closing the gap), turn.

Next row: Yo, knit to the 2 yo's, k3tog-tbl (the 2 yo's and next st on needle), turn.

Next row: B-yo, purl to the 2 yo's, p3tog (the 2 yo's and next st on needle), turn.

Rep last 2 rows until all yo pairs are worked.**

Last row: Yo, k12 (14, 16, 18) to center of heel.

FOOT

Join A and B.

Rnd 1: Beg chart and continue working both sole and instep as follows: N1: knit to yo; N2: Knit tog yo from N1 and first st on N2, then knit to last st, knit last st on N2 tog with the yo on N3; N3: knit across.

Work chart until foot measures approx 4½ (5¼, 7, 7½) inches or 1½ (1¾, 2, 2½) inches shorter than desired length,

ending with Rnd 10.

With A, knit 1 rnd.

Cut A and B, leaving 4-inch tails.

TOE

Work Toe with C.

Follow heel instructions from ** to **.

Last row (RS): Yo, k24 (28, 32, 36), leaving yo unworked—26 (30, 34, 38) sts on N1 [toe sts] and 24 (28, 32, 36) sts on N2 [instep sts].

Modified 3-Needle Bind-Off: With N1 and N2 parallel and WS tog, use a 3rd dpn to work bind-off as follows: N2: K2tog; N1: *p3tog (including yo), then pass first st over to bind off; N2: k2tog, then bind off st; N1: p2tog, then bind off st; rep from * until 3 sts (including yo) rem on N1, then p3tog and complete bind off.

FINISHING

Weave in all ends. Hand wash and block. ✪

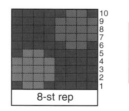

COLOR KEY
- A (Black)
- B (Hyacinth)
- C (Petal)

8-st rep

CHART

Diamond Swirl Socks

These socks feature an easy-to-memorize pattern of interlocking diamonds, adding flair to any outfit!

DESIGN BY SARAH WILSON

SIZES

Woman's small (large) to fit shoe sizes 5–7 (8–10) Instructions are given for smaller size, with larger size in parentheses. When only 1 number is given, it applies to both sizes.

FINISHED MEASUREMENTS

Circumference: 8 (9) inches
Foot length: 9 (10) inches

MATERIALS

- Colinette Yarns Jitterbug (sock weight/100% merino wool; 320 yds/100g per skein): 1 skein Gauguin #100
- Size 1 (2.25mm) double-pointed needles (set of 4) or size needed to obtain gauge
- Size E/4 (3.5mm) crochet hook

GAUGE

30 sts and 48 rnds = 4 inches/10 cm in St st.
To save time, take time to check gauge.

SPECIAL ABBREVIATIONS

Right Twist (RT): Knit 2nd st on LH needle, then knit first st, slipping both sts to RH needle.
Left Twist (LT): Knit 2nd st on LH needle tbl, then knit first st, slipping both sts to RH needle.

Increase 1 (Inc1): Knit into front and back of st.
N1, N2, N3: Needle 1, Needle 2, Needle 3
Wrap and Turn (W&T): Bring yarn to RS of work between needles, slip next st pwise to RH needle, bring yarn around this st to WS, slip st back to LH needle, turn work to begin working back in the other direction.
Work Wrapped Sts and Wraps Tog (WW): *On RS:* Knit to wrapped st, slip the wrapped st pwise from LH needle to RH needle. Use tip of LH needle to pick up wrap(s) and place it/them on RH needle. Slip wrap(s) and st back to LH needle and knit them tog.
On WS: Purl to wrapped st, slip the wrapped st kwise from LH needle to RH needle. Use tip of LH to pick up wrap(s) and place it/them on RH needle. Slip wrap(s) and st back to LH needle and purl them tog.

PATTERN STITCH

Interlocking Diamonds (multiple of 8 sts)
Rnd 1: *K1, p2, k2, p2, k1; rep from * around.
Rnd 2: *K1, p1, RT, LT, p1, k1; rep from * around.
Rnd 3: *K1, p1, k1, p2, k1, p1, k1; rep from * around.
Rnd 4: *K1, RT, p2, LT, k1; rep from * around.
Rnd 5: *K2, p4, k2; rep from * around.
Rnd 6: Knit.

Rnd 7: *K1, p2, k2, p2, k1; rep from * around.

Rnd 8: *LT, p1, k2, p1, RT; rep from * around.

Rnd 9: *P1, k1, p1, k2, p1, k1, p1; rep from * around.

Rnd 10: *P1, LT, k2, RT, p1; rep from * around.

Rnd 11: *P2, k4, p2; rep from * around.

Rnd 12: Knit.

Rep Rnds 1–12 for pat.

Provisional Cast-On: With crochet hook and waste yarn, make a chain several sts longer than desired cast on. With knitting needle and project yarn, pick up indicated number of sts in the "bumps" on back of chain. When indicated in pattern, "unzip" the crochet chain to free live sts.

This sock is worked on 3 double-pointed needles from the toe-up, with increased toe and short-row heel, ending with a picot bind-off on cuff.

A chart for the Interlocking Diamonds pattern is included for those preferring to work from charts.

Socks

Using provisional method, cast on 8 (12) sts.

Work 3 rows St st.

Remove waste yarn, placing sts on 2nd dpn (N1); place marker for beg of rnd—16 (24) sts.

Fold piece in half with WS tog and beg working in the rnd as follows:

Rnd 1: N1: Inc1, knit to last st, Inc1. N2: Inc1, knit to last st, Inc1—20 (28) sts.

Rnd 2: Knit.

Rep Rnds 1 and 2 until there are 64 (72) sts on needles, adding a 3rd dpn when needed to work with ease.

Distribute sts on needles as follows: N1 (½ instep): 16 (20) sts; N2 (½ instep): 16 (20) sts; N3 (sole): 32 sts.

Rnd 1: N1 and N2: Work Interlocking Diamonds pat across instep; N3: knit.

Work even in established pat until piece measures approx 7 (8) inches from beg, ending ready to work sts on N3.

Note: *Heel is worked back and forth across sts on N3.*

Row 1 (RS): Knit to last st, W&T.

Row 2: Purl to last st, W&T.

Row 3: Knit to st before last wrapped st, W&T.

Row 4: Purl to st before last wrapped st, W&T.

Rep Rows 3 and 4 until 10 sts rem unwrapped.

Row 5: Knit to the first wrapped st, WW, W&T.

Row 6: Purl to the first wrapped st, WW, W&T.

Row 7: Knit to the first double-wrapped st, WW, W&T.

Row 8: Purl to the first double-wrapped st, WW, W&T.

Row 9: Knit across.

Rep Rows 8 and 9 until all double-wrapped sts are worked and 32 sts are live.

LEG

Next 2 (4) rnds: N1 and N2: continue working in established pat, N3: knit.

Next rnd: Work Interlocking Diamonds pat around as established.

Work even until piece measures 6 inches from heel or 1 inch less than desired length.

Work 5 rnds in K1, P1 Rib.

PICOT EDGE BIND-OFF

*Cast on 1 st using cable method, k2, bind off 1 st, k2tog, bind off 1 st, then slip st on RH needle back to LH needle; rep from * until 1 st rem; cable cast on 1 st, k2, bind off 1 st; k1; bind off last st. Cut yarn and draw end through rem loop to finish.

FINISHING

Weave in all ends. Block. ✪

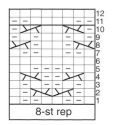

STITCH KEY

☐	Knit
—	Purl
⧖	RT
⧗	LT

INTERLOCKING DIAMONDS

Electric Flower Socks

This eye-catching design features beaded flowers arranged on a backdrop of bright yarn.

DESIGN BY ELLENE WARREN

◼◼◼◻ **INTERMEDIATE**

SIZES

Woman's small (medium/large) to fit shoe sizes 5–7 (8–10) Instructions are given for smaller size, with larger size in parentheses. When only 1 number is given, it applies to both sizes.

FINISHED MEASUREMENTS

Circumference: 8 (8¾) inches
Foot length: 9 (10) inches

MATERIALS

- Koigu KPM (fingering weight; 100% merino wool; 175 yds/50g per hank): 2 hanks bright yellow #1200
- Size 1 (2.25mm) double-pointed needles (set of 5) or size needed to obtain gauge
- Size D/3 (3.25mm) crochet hook
- 200 (240) multi-colored #6 glass seed beads
- Bead threader

1 SUPER FINE

GAUGE

30 sts and 36 rnds = 4 inches/10cm in St st.
To save time, take time to check gauge.

SPECIAL ABBREVIATIONS

Slip Bead (SB): Bring yarn forward as if to purl, move next bead up working yarn to sit snugly against work, slip next stitch pwise, return yarn to knitting position, leaving bead in front of slipped stitch.

N1, N2, N3, N4: Needle 1, Needle 2, Needle 3, Needle 4
Make 1 (M1): Insert LH needle from front to back under the running thread between the last st worked and next st on LH needle. With RH needle, knit into the back of this loop.

PATTERN STITCH

Bead Pat (multiple of 6 sts)
Rnds 1–3: Knit.
Rnd 4: *K3, SB, k1; rep from * around.
Rnd 5: *K2, SB, k1, SB, k1; rep from * around.
Rnd 6: Rep Rnd 4.
Rnds 7–9: Knit.
Rnd 10: *SB, k5; rep from * around.
Rnd 11: *K1, SB, k3, SB; rep from * around.
Rnd 12: Rep Rnd 10.
Rep Rnds 1–12 for pat.

PATTERN NOTES

Sock is worked on 4 double-pointed needles from the cuff down, with a flap heel, gusset and wedge toe.

For each sock, using the bead threader, thread half the beads onto 1 skein of yarn. As you work, unwind a small quantity of yarn, each time sliding the beads towards the ball until needed.

Socks

CUFF

Loosely cast on 60 (64) sts. Distribute sts evenly on 4 dpns; place marker for beg of

rnd and join, taking care not to twist sts.
  Work K2, P2 Rib for 1½ inches.
  On last rnd of larger size, inc as follows:
N1: Work rib; N2: M1, work rib to end; N3:
work rib, M1; N4: Work rib—60 (66) sts.

LEG

Work 5 (6) reps of Bead Pat, and on last
rnd of larger size, dec 1 st each on N2 and
N3—60 (64) sts.

HEEL FLAP

Row 1 (RS): Knit across N1, turn.
Row 2: Sl 1, purl across N1 and N4,
leaving rem sts on N2 and N3 (instep sts)
unworked.
Row 3: *Sl 1, k1; rep from * across, turn.
Row 4: Sl 1, purl across.
Row 5: Sl 1, *sl, k1; rep from * to last st, k1.
Row 6: Rep Row 4.
Rep [Rows 3–6] 6 (7) more times.

TURN HEEL

Row 1: (RS) K15 (16), ssk, k1, turn.
Row 2: Sl 1, p1, p2tog, p1, turn.
Row 3: Sl 1, k2, ssk, k1, turn.
Row 4: Sl 1, p3, p2tog, p1, turn.
  Continue working in this manner,
working 1 more st before dec on each

row, until all sts are worked; ***note:*** *on
larger size, do not work k1 (p1) following
dec on last 2 rows*—16 sts.

GUSSET

Set-up rnd: With spare dpn, sl 1, k7; with
N1, k8, then pick up and knit 15 (16) sts
along left side of flap; with N2 and N3,
knit across instep; with N4, pick up and
knit 15 (16) sts along right side of flap,
then k8 sts from spare dpn. Place marker
for beg of rnd at center of heel—66 (70)
sts divided as follows: 23 (24) sts on both
N1 and N4; 15 (16) sts on both N2 and N3.
Rnd 1: Knit around, knitting into back
loop of all picked-up sts.
Rnd 2 (dec): N1: Knit to last 3 sts, k2tog,
k1; N2 and 3: knit across; N4: k1, ssk, knit
to end.
Rnd 3: Knit around.
  Rep last 2 rnds until 60 (64) sts rem.

FOOT

Work even until foot measures 7 (8)
inches or approx 2 inches short of desired
length.

TOE

Dec rnd: *N1: Knit to last 3 sts, k2tog, k1;
N2: k1, ssk, knit to end; rep from * on N3
and 4—56 (60) sts.
  Rep Dec rnd [every other rnd] 4 (5)
times, then every rnd until 12 sts rem.
  Knit across N1.
  Cut yarn, leaving a 10-inch tail.
  Sl sts from N4 to N1 and from N3 to N2.
  Weave sts tog using Kitchener st (page 17).

FINISHING

Weave in all ends. Hand wash and block. ✪

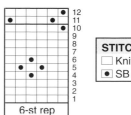

			12
			11
			10
			9
			8
			7
			6
			5
			4
			3
			2
			1

6-st rep

STITCH AND BEAD KEY
☐ Knit
⊡ SB

BEAD PATTERN

Fancy Fair Isle Socks

This versatile design features self-striping yarns to create impressive results.

DESIGN BY KATE ATHERLEY

■■■□ INTERMEDIATE

SIZES

Woman's small (woman's large, man's small, man's large) to fit woman's shoe sizes 5–7 (7½–9, man's shoe size 6–9, 9½–11) Instructions are given for smallest size, with larger sizes in parentheses. When only 1 number is given, it applies to all sizes.

FINISHED MEASUREMENTS

Circumference: 7½ (8, 8½, 9) inches
Foot length: 9 (10, 10, 11) inches

MATERIALS

- Schoeller + Stahl Fortissima Socka (sock weight; 60% superwash virgin wool/40% polypropylene; 213 yds/50g per ball): 2 balls charcoal grey #1410 (MC)
- Austermann Step (sock weight; 75% superwash virgin wool/25% nylon; 460 yds/100g per ball): 1 ball nordcap #0046 (CC)
- Size 1 (2.25mm) double-pointed needles (set of 5) or size needed to obtain gauge

1 SUPER FINE

GAUGE

30 sts and 42 rnds = 4 inches/10cm in both stranded St st and plain St st.
To save time, take time to check gauge.

SPECIAL ABBREVIATIONS

N1, N2, N3, N4: Needle 1, Needle 2, Needle 3, Needle 4

PATTERN NOTES

This sock is worked on 4 double-pointed needles from the cuff down, with a heel flap, gusset, and a wedge toe.

Work 2 gauge swatches and if necessary, go up in needle size for stranded stockinette stitch section.

Socks

CUFF & LEG

With MC, cast on 56 (60, 64, 68) sts.

Distribute sts evenly on 4 dpns; place marker for beg of rnd and join, taking care not to twists sts.

Work K1, P1 Rib for 1 inch.

Join CC and work Rnds 1–18 of chart 3 times.

Men's sizes only: Work Rnds 1–6 once more.

Cut CC yarn.

HEEL FLAP

Row 1 (RS): With MC, k14 (15, 16, 17), turn.
Row 2: Sl 1, p27 (29, 31, 33), turn, leaving rem sts on hold on N2 and N3 for instep.
Row 3: Sl 1, knit across heel sts.
Row 4: Sl 1, purl across heel sts.
Rep [last 2 rows] 8 (9, 10, 11) times.

TURN HEEL

Row 1 (RS): Sl 1, k18 (19, 20, 22), ssk, turn.
Row 2: Sl 1, p10 (10, 10, 12), p2tog, turn.
Row 3: Sl 1, k10 (10, 10, 12), ssk, turn.
Rep last 2 rows until all sts have been worked, ending with a WS row—12 (12, 12, 14) sts.

Set-up rnd: With a spare dpn, sl 1, k5 (5, 6); with N1, k6 (6, 6, 7), then pick up and knit 14 (15, 16, 17) sts along left side of flap; with N2 and N3, knit across instep; with N4, pick up and knit 14 (15, 16, 17) sts along right side of flap, then k6 (6, 6, 7) sts from spare dpn. Place marker for beg of rnd in center of heel—68 (72, 76, 82) sts divided as follows: 20 (21, 22, 24) sts on both N1 and N4; 14 (15, 16, 17) sts on both N2 and N3.

Rnd 1: Knit around, knitting into back loop of all picked-up sts.

Rnd 2 (dec): N1: Knit to last 3 sts, k2tog, k1; N2 and 3: knit across; N4: k1, ssk, knit to end.

Rnd 3: Knit around.

Rep last 2 rnds until 56 (60, 64, 68) sts rem with 14 (15, 16, 17) sts on each needle.

FOOT

Work even until foot measures 7 (8, 8, 9) inches or approx 2 inches short of desired length.

```
18
17
16
15
14
13
12
11
10
9
8
7
6
5
4
3
2
1
4-st rep
```

COLOR KEY
■ MC
■ CC

CHART

TOE

Dec rnd: *N1: Knit to last 3 sts, k2tog, k1; N2: k1, ssk, knit to end; rep from * on N3 and 4—52 (56, 60, 64) sts.

Rep Dec rnd [every 4 rnds] once, [every 3 rnds] twice, [every other rnd] 3 times, then every rnd until 8 sts rem with 2 sts on each needle.

Cut yarn, leaving a 6-inch tail.

Using tapestry needle, thread tail through rem sts, and pull tight and secure on WS.

FINISHING

Weave in all ends. Block. ✪

Tickle Your Toes
Top-Down Socks

Your little one will look too cute in these top-down socks!

DESIGN BY SUSAN ROBICHEAU

INTERMEDIATE

SIZES

Child's small (medium, large) to fit child's shoe sizes 6½–7 (8–8½, 9–10) Instructions are given for smallest size, with larger sizes in parentheses. When only 1 number is given, it applies to all sizes.

FINISHED MEASUREMENTS

Circumference: 6¼ inches
Foot length: 5½ (6, 6½) inches

MATERIALS

- Schaefer Yarn Heather (sock weight; 55% merino superwash wool/30% cultivated silk/15% nylon; 400 yds/4 oz per skein): 1 skein Tink

1 SUPER FINE

- 2 size 2 (2.75mm) circular needles or size needed to obtain gauge
- Stitch marker

GAUGE

32 sts and 36 rnds = 4 inches/10cm in St st.
To save time, take time to check gauge.

SPECIAL ABBREVIATIONS

N1, N2: Needle 1 (heel and sole sts), needle 2. (instep sts)

PATTERN STITCHES

Faux Cable Rib in the round (multiple of 5 sts)

Rnds 1 and 2: *P1, k3, p1; rep from * around.
Rnd 3: *P1, sk2p, p1; rep from * around.
Rnd 4: *P1, (k1, p1, k1) in next st, p1; rep from * around.
  Rep Rnds 1–4 for pat.

Faux Cable Rib worked flat
(multiple of 5 sts)
Row 1 (RS): P1, k3, p1.
Row 2: K2, p3, k1.
Row 3: P1, sk2p, p1.
Row 4: K1, (p1, k1, p1) in next st, k1.
  Rep Rows 1–4 for pat.

PATTERN NOTE

This sock is worked on 2 circular needles from the cuff down with a heel flap, gusset and wedge toe.

Socks

CUFF

Using cable method, cast on 50 sts.
  Place 25 sts on each needle; place marker for beg of rnd and join, taking care not to twist sts.
  Work 3 (3, 4) reps of Faux Cable Rib.

LEG

Set-up rnd: N1: Work pat as established over first 6 sts, knit to last 6 sts, work pat as established over last 6 sts; N2: work as for N1.

Work even in established pat for 24 (28, 28) rnds [6 (7, 7) reps of rib pat].

HEEL FLAP

Working back and forth on N1 sts only, work 18 rows in established pat, with sts on N2 on hold for instep.

TURN HEEL

Row 1 (RS): K16, ssk, turn.
Row 2: Sl 1, p7, p2tog.
Row 3: Sl 1, k7, ssk.

Rep Rows 2 and 3 until all sts have been worked, ending with Row 2—9 sts rem.

GUSSET

Set-up rnd: N1: Knit across 9 heel sts, pick up and knit 9 sts along left side of flap, then pick up and knit 1 st in row below first instep st on N2 (this will prevent a hole); N2: work in established pat across 25 instep sts; N1: pick up and knit 1 st in row below last instep st on N2, then pick up and knit 9 sts along right side of heel flap, knit across rem sts of N1; N2: work in established pat across; place marker for beg of rnd—54 sts with 29 sts on N1 and 25 sts on N2.

Dec rnd: N1: K1, ssk, knit to last 3 sts, k2tog, k1; N2: work even in established pat—52 sts.
Rnd 2: Work even.

Rep Dec rnd once more—50 sts.

FOOT

Work even until foot measures approx 4 (4½, 5) inches from back of heel, ending with Rnd 4 of rib pat.

TOE

Rnd 1 (dec): N1: K5, ssk, knit to last 7 sts, k2tog, k5; N2: work 5 sts in pat, ssk, knit to last 7 sts, k2tog, work 5 sts in pat—46 sts.
Rnd 2: Work even.

Rep [Rnds 1 and 2] 4 times—30 sts.

Rep [Rnd 1] twice more—22 sts with 11 sts on each needle.
Last rnd: N1: K5, k2tog, k4; N2: p1, k4, k2tog, k3, p1—20 sts.

Using Kitchener stitch (page 17), graft sts from N1 and N2 tog.

FINISHING

Weave in ends. Block. ✪

Foot Fetish Socks

Indulge your "fetish" with this enticing twisted rib pattern that continues through the leg and foot.

DESIGN BY ELLENE WARREN

 INTERMEDIATE

SIZES

Woman's small (medium/large) to fit shoe sizes 5–7 (8–10) Instructions are given for smaller size, with larger size in parentheses. When only 1 number is given, it applies to both sizes.

FINISHED MEASUREMENTS

Circumference: 6 (7) inches (unstretched)
Foot length: 9 (10) inches

MATERIALS

- Koigu KPM (sport weight; 100% merino wool; 175 yds/50g per hank): 2 (3) hanks medium blue #2326
- Size 0 (2mm) double-pointed needles (set of 4) or size needed to obtain gauge (for size small)
- Size 2 (2.75mm) double-pointed needles (set of 4) or size needed to obtain gauge (for size medium/large)

GAUGE

Small: 44 sts and 36 rnds = 4 inches/10cm in Fetish Lace pat (unstretched) with smaller needles.
Medium: 38 sts and 34 rnds = 4 inches/10cm in Fetish Lace pat (unstretched) with larger needles.
To save time, take time to check gauge.

SPECIAL ABBREVIATIONS

Left Cross (LC): Slip next 2 sts to RH pwise then return sts to LH needle by inserting its tip pwise from right to left into the 2 transferred sts at the same time; k2.

N1, N2, N3: Needle 1, needle 2, needle 3
Make 1 (M1): Insert LH needle from front to back under the running thread between the last st worked and next st on LH needle. With RH needle, knit into the back of this loop.

PATTERN STITCHES

Cuff Rib (multiple of 11 sts)
Rnd 1: *P2, [k1-tbl, p1] twice, k1-tbl, p2, k2; rep from * around.
Rnd 2: *P2, [k1-tbl, p1] twice, k1-tbl, p2, LC; rep from * around.
 Rep Rnds 1 and 2 for pat.

Fetish Lace (multiple of 11 sts)
Rnd 1: *P2, yo, ssk, k1, k2tog, yo, p2, LC; rep from * around.
Rnd 2: *P2, k5, p2, k2; rep from * around.
Rnd 3: *P2, k1, yo, sk2p, yo, k1, p2, LC; rep from * around.
Rnd 4: Rep Rnd 2.
 Rep Rnds 1–4 for pat.

PATTERN NOTES

This sock is worked on 3 dpns from the cuff down with heel flap, gussets and wedge toe.

 The pat is worked on the same st count for both sizes, but the needle size and st gauge are different, as is the measurement of the lengths of the leg and foot.

Socks

CUFF

Cast on 66 sts; distribute evenly onto 3 dpns, place marker for beg of rnd and join, taking care not to twist sts.

Work Cuff Rib for 1½ inches, ending with Rnd 1.

LEG

Work Fetish Lace until piece measures 7 (7½) inches from beg, ending with Rnd 4.

HEEL FLAP

Set-up Row 1 (RS): P2, yo, ssk, k1, k2tog, yo, p2, turn. Slip rem 13 sts on needle to another dpn to hold for instep.

Set-up Row 2: P31.

Row 1: Working back and forth on 31 heel sts only, sl 1, *k1, sl 1; rep from * to last 2 sts, k2.

Rows 2 and 4: Sl 1, purl across.

Row 3: Sl 1, k2, *sl 1, k1; rep from * to end.

Rep [Rows 1–4] 7 times.

TURN HEEL

Row 1 (RS): Sl 1, k15, ssk, k1, turn.

Row 2: Sl 1, p2, p2tog, p1, turn.

Row 3: Sl 1, knit to 1 st before gap, ssk, k1, turn.

Row 4: Sl 1, purl to 1 st before gap, p2tog, p1, turn.

Rep Rows 3 and 4 until all heel flap sts have been worked, ending on a WS row, turn—17 sts.

Next Row: Sl 1, k8, do not turn.

GUSSET

Set-up Rnd: With N1, k8, then pick up and knit 16 sts along edge of heel flap, M1 in running thread between heel and instep sts; with N2, work in established pat across 35 instep sts; with N3, M1 in running thread between heel and instep sts, then pick up and knit 15 sts along edge of heel flap, k9—85 sts distributed as follows: N1: 25 sts; N2: 35 sts; N3: 25 sts.

Rnd 1: N1: Knit to last 3 sts, k2tog, k1; N2: work in established pat; N3: k1, ssk, knit to end of rnd—83 sts.

Rnd 2: N1: Knit; N2: work in established pat; N3: knit.

Rep Rnds 1 and 2 until 16 sts rem on N1 and N3—67 sts.

FOOT

Rnd 1: N1: Knit; N2: work in established pat; N3: knit.

Work even until foot measures 7 (8) inches from heel or 2 inches short of desired length, ending with Rnd 4.

TOE

Set-up Rnd: N1: Knit; N2: ssk, k15, k2tog, knit to last 2 sts, k2tog; N3: knit—64 sts.

Rnd 1: N1: Knit to last 3 sts, k2tog, k1; N2: k1, ssk, knit to last 3 sts, k2tog, k1; N3: k1, ssk, knit to end—60 sts.

Rnd 2: Knit.

Rep Rnds 1 and 2 until 24 sts rem.

With N3, k6 from N1—12 sts each on N2 and N3.

Cut yarn, leaving a 10-inch tail.

Graft toe sts using Kitchener st (pg. 17).

FINISHING

Weave in all ends. Block lightly. ✿

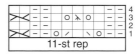

FETISH LACE

STITCH KEY	
−	Purl
o	Yo
╲	Ssk
☐	Knit
╱	K2tog
✕	LC
☀	Sk2p

Zany Zigzag Socks

These delightful socks feature a whimsical stitch pattern that's easy to memorize and is suitable for both men and women alike.

DESIGN BY SARAH WILSON

■■■■ EXPERIENCED

SIZES
Woman's small (large) to fit shoe sizes 5–7 (8–10) Instructions are given for smaller size, with larger size in parentheses. When only 1 number is given, it applies to both sizes.

FINISHED MEASUREMENTS
Circumference: 8 (9) inches
Foot length: 9 (10) inches

MATERIALS
- Plymouth Happy Feet (sock weight; 90% superwash merino wool/10% nylon; 192 yds/50g per skein: 2 skeins grape/garnet #5
- Size 1 (2.5mm) double-pointed needles (set of 4) or size needed to obtain gauge

1 SUPER FINE

GAUGE
34 sts and 52 rnds = 4 inches/10cm in St st.
To save time, take time to check gauge.

SPECIAL ABBREVIATIONS
Lifted Increase (L1): Use tip of RH needle to lift purl bump below the next st on LH needle, placing it onto LH needle; knit this st, then knit the next st on needle.
N1, N2, N3: Needle 1, Needle 2, Needle 3
Wrap and Turn (W&T): Bring yarn to RS of work between needles, slip next st pwise to RH needle, bring yarn around this st to WS, slip st back to LH needle, turn work to begin working back in the other direction.

PATTERN STITCHES
Cuff Rib (multiple of 11 sts)
Rnd 1: *K4, p2, k3, p2; rep from * around.
Rep Rnd 1 for pat.

Zigzag Pat (multiple of 11 sts)
Rnd 1: *L1, k2, ssk, k6; rep from * around.
Rnd 2 (and all even rnds): Knit.
Rnd 3: *K1, L1, k2, ssk, k5; rep from * around.
Rnd 5: *K2, L1, k2, ssk, k4; rep from * around.
Rnd 7: *K3, L1, k2, ssk, k4; rep from * around.
Rnd 9: *K4, L1, k2, ssk, k2; rep from * around.
Rnd 11: *K5, L1, k2, ssk, k1; rep from * around.
Rnd 13: *K6, L1, k2, ssk; rep from * around.
Rnd 15: *K6, k2tog, k2, L1; rep from * around.
Rnd 17: *K5, k2tog, k2, L1, k1; rep from * around.
Rnd 19: *K4, k2tog, k2, L1, k2; rep from * around.
Rnd 21: *K3, k2tog, k2, L1, k3; rep from * around.
Rnd 23: *K2, *k2tog, k2, L1, k4; rep from * around.

Rnd 25: *K1, *k2tog, k2, L1, k5; rep from * around.

Rnd 27: *k2tog, k2, L1, k6; rep from * around.

Rnd 28: Knit.

Rep Rnds 1–28 for pat.

Hiding wraps: On RS rows, pick up wrap from front to back and knit tog with wrapped st. On WS rows, pick up wrap from the back, then purl it tog with wrapped st.

PATTERN NOTES

This sock is worked on 3 double-pointed needles from the cuff down, with a heel flap and gusset and wedge toe.

The number of stitches on Needles 1 and 3 will vary as you work the Zigzag Pattern but the total stitch count for each round will remain the same, i.e. 66 (77) stitches.

Socks

CUFF

Cast on 66 (77) sts.
Distribute sts as follows: N1: 14 (22) sts; N2: 33 sts; N3: 19 (22)

sts; place marker for beg of rnd and join, taking care not to twist sts.

Work 12 rnds of Cuff Rib.

Work 2½ reps of Zigzag pat, ending at Rnd 13.

HEEL FLAP

Set-up row: N1: K22; N2: k33 (sts will need to be rearranged for smaller size). Heel flap will be worked flat across these 33 sts, with rem sts held on dpns for instep.

Work in established pat on 33 heel flap sts, purling on WS rows and ending on Row 14.

TURN HEEL

Row 1 (RS): K20, W&T.

Row 2 (WS): P7, W&T.

Row 3: Knit to wrapped st, hide wrap, W&T.

Row 4: Purl to wrapped st, hide wrap, W&T.

Rep Rows 3 and 4 until all sts are worked and first and last sts are wrapped.

GUSSET

Note: Needle numbers are reassigned as N1 and N3: sole sts and N2: instep sts.

Set-up rnd: With N1, knit across heel sts (hiding last wrap), pick up and knit 14 sts along edge of heel flap, and 1 st between top of heel flap and instep sts; with N2, work established Zigzag pat across 33 (44) instep sts; with N3, pick up and knit 1 st between instep sts and top of heel flap, and 14 sts along edge of heel flap, k17 from N1 (hiding wrap on first st); place marker for beg of rnd—96 (107) sts distributed as follows: N1: 31 sts, N2: 33 (44) sts, N3: 32 sts.

Rnd 2: N1: Knit; N2: work in established pat; N3: knit.

Rnd 3: N1: Knit to last 2 sts, k2tog; N2: work in pat; N3: ssk, knit to end— 94 (105) sts.

Rep Rnds 2 and 3 until there are 16 sts on N1 and 17 sts on N3—66 (77) sts.

FOOT

Work even, working instep sts in Zigzag pat and sole sts in St st until foot measures 7½ (8½) inches from back of heel.

For larger size only

Rearrange sts as follows: N1: 20 sts; N2: 38 sts; N3: 19 sts.

Next rnd: N1: Knit to last 3 sts, k2tog, k1; N2 and N3: knit—76 sts.

TOE

For both sizes

Rnd 1: Knit.

Rnd 2 (dec): N1: Knit to last 3 sts, k2tog, k1; N2: k1, ssk, knit to last 3 sts, k2tog, k1; N3: k1, ssk, knit to end—62 (72) sts.

Rep Rnds 1 and 2 until 26 (28) sts rem.

With N3, knit sts on N1—13 (14) sts on each needle.

Cut yarn, leaving a 16-inch tail.

Graft toe using Kitchener st (page 17).

FINISHING

Weave in all ends. Block as desired. ✪

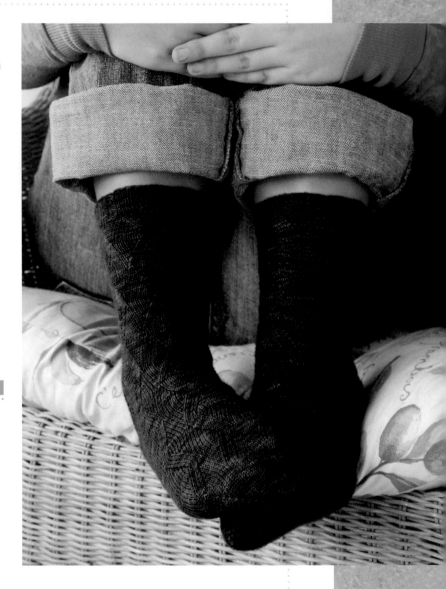

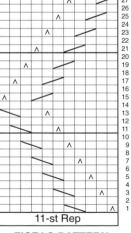

ZIGZAG PATTERN

11-st Rep

STITCH KEY

∧	L1
⟍	Ssk
☐	Knit
⟋	K2tog

Bahama Mama Flip-Flop Socks

Add some fun to your flip-flops while wearing these whimsical split-toe socks!

DESIGN BY SEAN HIGGINS

▰▰▰▱ INTERMEDIATE

SIZES

Woman's small (large) to fit shoe sizes 5–7 (8–10) Instructions are given for the smaller size, with larger size in parentheses. When only 1 number is given, it applies to both sizes.

FINISHED MEASUREMENTS

Circumference: 6½ (7¼) inches (see Pattern Notes)
Foot length: 9 (9¾) inches

MATERIALS

- Cascade Fixation Effects (DK weight; 98.3% cotton/1.7% elastic; 100 yds/50g per ball): 2 (3) balls green #9385
- Size 3 (3.25 mm) double-pointed and 32-inch circular needles or size needed to obtain gauge

3 LIGHT

GAUGE

30 sts and 13 rnds = 4 inches/10 cm in St st.
36 sts and 13 rnds = 4 inches/10 cm in Lace Rib pat.
To save time, take time to check gauge.

SPECIAL ABBREVIATIONS

Knit in front and back (kf&b): Inc 1 st by knitting in front and back of same st.
N1, N2: Needle 1 (instep sts), Needle 2 (sole sts)

Wrap and Turn (W&T): Bring yarn to RS of work between needles, slip next st pwise to RH needle, bring yarn around this st to WS, slip st back to LH needle, turn work to begin working back in the other direction.
Work wrapped sts and wraps tog (WW): *On RS:* Knit to wrapped st, slip the wrapped st pwise from LH needle to RH needle. Use tip of LH needle to pick up wrap(s) and place it/them on RH needle. Slip wrap(s) and st back to LH needle and knit them tog.
On WS: Purl to wrapped st, slip the wrapped st kwise from LH needle to RH needle. Use tip of LH to pick up wrap(s) and place it/them on RH needle. Slip wrap(s) and st back to LH needle and purl them tog.

PATTERN STITCHES

Lace Rib (multiple of 6 sts)
Rnds 1 and 3: *K2, p1; rep from * around.
Rnd 2: *K2, p1, yo, ssk, p1; rep from * around.
Rnd 4: *K2, p1, k2tog, yo, p1; rep from * around.
   Rep Rnds 1–4 for pat.

Twisted Rib (multiple of 2 sts)
Rnd 1: *K1-tbl, p1; rep from * around.
   Rep Rnd 1 for pat.

SPECIAL TECHNIQUES

3-Needle Bind-Off: With RS tog and

needles parallel, using a 3rd needle, knit tog 1 st from the front needle with 1 from the back. *Knit tog 1 st from the front and back needles, and slip the first st over the 2nd to bind off. Rep from * until required number of sts are bound off.

Picot Bind-Off: *Cast on 3 sts using the cable method. Bind off 6 sts. Slip the rem st on the RH needle back to the LH needle. Rep from * around to last st, fasten off last st and weave in end next to beg-of-rnd st to close circle.

PATTERN NOTES

This sock is worked from the toe up (with big toe separated from other 4 toes), has a short-row heel and ends with a Picot Bind-Off.

It begins with a Turkish cast-on (page 10) on double-pointed needles and when there are enough stitches, they are transferred to 1 long needle (Magic Loop method); the pattern can also be easily read for working with 2 circular needles.

The sock is deliberately knit to be snug to allow for stretch of the lace rib pattern.

Elastic yarn knits up at different gauge and yardage based upon tension; use a firm tension on the yarn when knitting.

Socks

BIG TOE

Using Turkish Cast-On (page 10) and 2 dpns, cast on 6 sts (3 sts each needle).
Rnd 1: With 3rd dpn, knit across sts on each needle; mark beg of rnd.
Rnd 2: N1 and N2: [Kf&b] twice, k1—10 sts with 5 on each needle.
Rnd 3 and all odd numbered rnds: Knit even on both needles.
Rnd 4: N1 and N2: [Kf&b] 4 times, k1—18 sts with 9 on each needle.
Rnd 6: N1 and N2: Kf&b, k6, kf&b, k1—22 sts with 11 on each needle.

Rnd 7: Knit even on both needles.
For size large only:
Rnd 8: N1 and N2: Kf&b, k8, kf&b, k1—26 sts with 13 on each needle.
For both sizes:
Work even in St st until piece measures 2 inches or reaches the base of your toe; cut yarn.

Slip sts from N1 and N2 to separate pieces of waste yarn and set aside.

4-TOE SECTION

Work as for Big Toe through Rnd 7 (both sizes)—22 sts with 11 on each needle.
Rnd 8: N1 and N2: [Kf&b, k2] 3 times, kf&b, k1—30 sts with 15 on each needle.
Rnd 9: Knit even on both needles.
Rnd 10: N1: Kf&b, knit to end; N2: knit to last 2 sts, kf&b, k1—32 sts with 16 on each needle.
Rnd 11: Knit all sts.
Rep [Rnds 10 and 11] 6 (7) more times—44 (46) sts with 22 (23) on each needle.

Slip these sts to long circular needle (half the sts on each end of needle [now N1 and N2]) and beg working following Magic Loop method.

Work even in St st until piece measures 2 inches or reaches base of toes.

Rnd 1: Slip last and first 4 sts of big-toe to dpn, leaving rem 14 (18) sts on waste yarn; N1: k18 (19); pull needle/cable of circular needle so that 4 rem sts transfer to N2; N2: using 3-Needle Bind-Off, bind off next 8 sts tog with 8 big toe sts on dpn; k18 (19) sts—50 (56) sts, with 36 (38) sts in 4-toe section and 14 (18) sts in big-toe section.

Rnd 2: N1: K18 (19), pick up and knit 2 sts at join; sl 7 (9) sts from waste yarn onto LH needle and knit them; N2: Sl last 7 (9) sts from waste yarn onto LH needle and knit them; pick up and knit 2 sts at join, k18 (19)—54 (60) sts with 27 (30) sts each needle.

Knit 2 rnds.

Set up Lace Rib pat:

Rnds 1 and 3: N1: *K2, p1; rep from * to end; N2: knit.

Rnd 2: N1: small: *k2, p1, yo, ssk, p1; rep from * to last 3 sts, end k2, p1; (large: *k2, p1, yo, ssk, p1; rep from * to end); N2: knit.

Rnd 4: N1: small: *k2, p1, k2tog, p1; rep from * to last 3 sts, end k2, p1; (large: *k2,

p1, k2tog, p1; rep from * to end); N2: knit.

Work even in established Lace Rib (N1) and St st (N2) until foot measures 7½ (8¼) inches from tip of big toe, ending with N1: Rnd 2 or 4.

Heel is worked back and forth over N2 sts only; instep sts will rem on hold on cable of circular needle.

Row 1: Knit to last st, W&T.

Row 2: Purl to last st, W&T.

Row 3: Knit to first unwrapped st, W&T.

Row 4: Purl to first unwrapped st, W&T.

Rep Rows 3 and 4 until 7 (8) sts are wrapped on each side—13 (14) sts in center rem unwrapped.

Row 5: Knit to first wrapped st, WW, W&T.

Row 6: Purl to first wrapped st, WW, W&T.

Row 7: Knit to first double-wrapped st, WW, W&T.

Row 8: Purl to first double-wrapped st, WW, W&T.

Rep Rows 7 and 8 until 1 double-wrapped st rem at each end of N2.

Knit to double-wrapped st, WW; do not turn—1 double-wrapped st rem at beg of N2.

Continue in the round.

N1: Work in established Lace Rib; N2: WW, knit to end.

Beg working established Lace Rib pat all around.

Note: *For size small, if desired for ease of working pat, rearrange sts so that there are 30 sts on N1 and 24 on N2.*

Work even until leg measures 4½ (5¼) inches from bottom of heel, ending with Rnd 1 or 3.

Work 1½ inches in Twisted Rib.

Using Picot Bind-Off, bind off all sts.

Weave in ends. Block.✪

Twisted Rib "Reversi" Socks

Get two looks in one with these reversible socks. This easy to memorize pattern will compliment any wardrobe.

DESIGN BY KATHRYN BECKERDITE

◨◼◼◻ INTERMEDIATE

SIZES

Woman's small (woman's large, man's small, man's large) to fit woman's shoe size 6–7 (woman's 8–9, man's shoe size 8–9, man's 10–11) Instructions are given for smallest size, with larger sizes in parentheses. When only 1 number is given, it applies to all sizes.

FINISHED MEASUREMENTS

Circumference: 7½ (8, 8½, 9) inches
Foot length: 9 (9¾, 10½, 11¼) inches

MATERIALS

- Brown Sheep Company Wildfoote Luxury (sock weight; 75% washable wool/25% nylon; 215 yds/50g per skein): 3 (3, 4, 4) skeins bark cloth #SY12 (MC); 1 skein pine tree # SY27 (CC)

① SUPER FINE

- Size 1 (2.25mm) double-pointed needles (set of 5) or size needed to obtain gauge
- Stitch marker

GAUGE

36 sts and 44 rnds = 4 inches/10cm in St st.
To save time, take time to check gauge.

SPECIAL ABBREVIATIONS

N1, N2, N3, N4: Needle 1, Needle 2, Needle 3, Needle 4

Wrap and Turn (W&T): Bring yarn to RS of work between needles, slip next st pwise to RH needle, bring yarn around this st to WS, slip st back to LH needle, turn work to begin working back in the other direction.

Work wrapped sts and wraps tog (WW): *On RS:* Knit to wrapped st, slip the wrapped st pwise from LH needle to RH needle. Use tip of LH needle to pick up wrap(s) and place it/them on RH needle. Slip wrap(s) and st back to LH needle and knit them tog.
On WS: Purl to wrapped st, slip the wrapped st kwise from LH needle to RH needle. Use tip of LH to pick up wrap(s) and place it/them on RH needle. Slip wrap(s) and st back to LH needle and purl them tog.

Make 1 (M1): Insert LH needle from front to back under the running thread between the last st worked and next st on LH needle. With RH needle, knit into the back of this loop.

Right Twist (RT): K2tog but do not drop sts from LH needle, knit again into first st on LH needle, drop both sts from LH needle.

Left Twist (LT): Bring RH needle behind

through. Drop the first st off the needle. Rep from * around.

These socks are worked on 4 double-pointed needles from the toe up with short-row toe and heel shaping and ending with a Sewn Bind-Off.

Instep stitches are on Needle 1 and Needle 2; sole stitches are on Needle 3 and Needle 4.

First Sock

SHORT-ROW TOE

Using provisional method and MC, cast on 36 (40, 44, 48) sts.
Row 1 (WS): Purl.
Row 2: Knit to last st, W&T.
Row 3: Purl to last st, W&T.
Row 4: Knit to st before last wrapped st, W&T.
Row 5: Purl to st before last wrapped st, W&T.
Rep Rows 4 and 5 until 14 (16, 18, 20) sts rem unwrapped.
Row 6 (RS): Purl to the first wrapped st, WW, W&T.
Row 7: Knit to the first wrapped st, WW, W&T.
Row 8: Purl to the first double-wrapped st, WW, W&T.
Row 9: Knit to the first double-wrapped st, WW, W&T.
Rep Rows 8 and 9 until 2 double-wrapped sts rem (1 at each end).
Row 10 (RS): Purl across, WW, place marker for beg of rnd.
Unzip Provisional Cast-On and distribute newly live (instep) sts and sole sts evenly divided on 4 dpns—72 (80, 88, 96) sts with 18 (20, 22, 24) sts on each needle.

FOOT INSTEP

Rnd 1 (inc instep sts): N1 and N2: [K4, M1] 8 (9, 10, 11) times, k4; N3 and N4:

LH needle and knit into back of 2nd st on LH needle without dropping st from needle; knit into front of first st on LH needle, drop both stitches from LH needle.

PATTERN STITCH

Twisted Rib (multiple of 5 sts)
Rnd 1: *P1, RT, p1, k1; rep from * to end.
Rnds 2–4: *P1, k2, p1, k1; rep from * to end.
Rep Rnds 1–4 for pat for first sock.
On 2nd sock, work LT instead of RT.

SPECIAL TECHNIQUES

Provisional Cast-On: With crochet hook and waste yarn, make a chain several sts longer than desired cast on. With knitting needle and project yarn, pick up indicated number of sts in the "bumps" on back of chain. When indicated in pat, "unzip" the crochet chain to free live sts.
Sewn Bind-Off: Cut yarn leaving a 1-yd tail. Using a tapestry needle, *thread the yarn pwise through the first 2 sts on the needle. Pull through, leaving the sts on the needle. Thread the yarn kwise through the first st on the needle, pull

WW last double-wrapped st, purl to end of rnd—80 (89, 99, 107) sts with 44 (49, 54, 59) sts on N1 and N2 and 36 (40, 44, 48) sts on N3 and N4.

Rnd 2 (set-up rnd): N1 and N2: [P1, RT, p1, k1] 8 (9, 10, 11) times, p1, RT, p1; N3 and N4: purl to end of rnd.

Work even in established pats (Twisted Rib on N1 and N2 and rev St st on N3 and N4) until piece measures 7 (7½, 8¼, 8¾) inches or approx 2 (2¼, 2¼, 2½) inches short of desired length and ending with Rnd 2 of Twisted Rib; turn after completing last rnd.

HEEL

Row 1 (WS): K36 (40, 44, 48), turn, leaving instep sts on hold on N1 and N2.

Row 2 (RS): Purl to last st, W&T.

Row 3: Knit to last st, W&T.

Row 4: Purl to st before last wrapped st, W&T.

Row 5: Knit to st before last wrapped st, W&T.

Rep Rows 4 and 5 until 14 (16, 18, 20) sts rem unwrapped.

Row 6: Purl to the first wrapped st, WW, W&T.

Row 7: Knit to the first wrapped st, WW, W&T.

Row 8: Purl to the first double-wrapped st, WW, W&T.

Row 9: Knit to the first double-wrapped st, pickup wraps, WW, W&T.

Rep Rows 8 and 9 until 2 double-wrapped sts rem (1 at each end).

Row 10: Purl to double-wrapped st, WW, do not turn.

LEG

Rnd 1: N1 and N2: Work in established rib; N3 and N4: WW, purl to end.

Rnd 2 (inc): N1 and N2: Work in established rib; N3 and N4: [M1, p1, k2, p1] 9 (10, 11, 12) times, end M1—90 (100, 110, 120) sts with 44 (49, 54, 59) sts on N2 and N2 and 46 (51, 56, 61) sts on N3 and N4.

Work even in established Twisted Rib all around until leg measures approx 11¾ (12¼, 13½, 14¼) inches or desired length to cuff.

CUFF

Change to CC and continue in Twisted Rib for approx 2½ (3, 4, 4¼) inches or desired length of cuff, ending with Rnd 4.

Work Rnd 2 once more.

FINISHING

Bind off using sewn bind-off. Weave in ends.

Second Sock

Make a 2nd sock, substituting LT for RT in Twisted Rib. ✪

Little Tike Toe-Up Socks

Kiddies' feet will stay warm in these eye-catching socks.

DESIGN BY NAZANIN S. FARD

◀▬■■■▭ *INTERMEDIATE*

SIZES

Child's small (medium) Instructions are given for smaller size, with larger size in parentheses. When only 1 number is given, it applies to both sizes.

FINISHED MEASUREMENT

Circumference: 5 (6½) inches
Foot length: 5 (7) inches

MATERIALS

- Zitron Trekking XXL (sock weight; 75% new wool/25% nylon; 459 yds/100g per ball): 1 ball self-striping brights #311

  1 SUPER FINE

- 2 size 3 (3.25mm) 24-inch circular needles or size needed to obtain gauge
- Size F/5 (3.75mm) crochet hook

GAUGE

28 sts and 36 rnds = 4 inches/10cm in St st. To save time, take time to check gauge.

SPECIAL ABBREVIATIONS

N1, N2: Needle 1 (sole), needle 2 (instep)
Wrap and Turn (W&T): Bring yarn to RS of work between needles, slip next st pwise to RH needle, bring yarn around this st to WS, slip st back to LH needle, turn work to begin working back in the other direction.
Work wrapped sts and wraps tog (WW):
On RS: Knit to wrapped st, slip the wrapped st pwise from LH needle to RH needle. Use tip of LH needle to pick up wrap(s) and place it/them on RH needle. Slip wrap(s) and st back to LH needle and knit them tog.
On WS: Purl to wrapped st, slip the wrapped st kwise from LH needle to RH needle. Use tip of LH to pick up wrap(s) and place it/them on RH needle. Slip wrap(s) and st back to LH needle and purl them tog.
Make 1 Left (M1L): Insert LH needle from front to back under the running thread between the last st worked and next st on LH needle. With RH needle, knit into the back of this loop.
Make 1 Right (M1R): Insert LH needle from back to front under the running thread between the last st worked and next st on LH needle. With RH needle, knit into the front of this loop.

PATTERN STITCH

Eyelet Rib (multiple of 5 sts + 2)
Rnd 1: P2, *k3, p2; rep from * to end.
Rnd 2: P2, *k1, yo, k2tog, p2; rep from * to end.
Rnds 3 and 4: Rep Rnd 1.
  Rep Rnds 1–4 for pat.
Note: *When working all-around for leg, work established 5-st rep only.*

SPECIAL TECHNIQUE

Provisional Cast-On: With crochet hook and waste yarn, make a chain several sts longer than desired cast on. With knitting needle and project yarn, pick up indicated number of sts in the "bumps" on back of chain. When indicated in pattern, "unzip" the crochet chain to free live sts.

PATTERN NOTES

This sock is worked on 2 circular needles

from the toe up, with a short-row toe, a gusset and a short-row heel.

A chart for Eyelet Rib pattern is included for those preferring to work from charts.

One ball of yarn will make 3 pairs of small-sized socks and 2 pairs of medium-sized socks.

Socks

TOE

Using provisional method and 1 circular needle (N1), cast on 18 (23) sts.
Row 1 (WS): Purl.
Row 2: Knit to last st, W&T.
Row 3: Purl to last st, W&T.
Row 4: Knit to st before last wrapped st, W&T.
Row 5: Purl to st before last wrapped st, W&T.
Rep Rows 4 and 5 until 6 (11) sts rem unwrapped.
Row 6: Knit to the first wrapped st, WW, W&T.
Row 7: Purl to the first wrapped st, WW, W&T.
Row 8: Knit to the first double-wrapped st, WW, W&T.
Row 9: Purl to the first double-wrapped st, WW, W&T.
Rep Rows 8 and 9 until 1 double-wrapped st rem at each end of work.

FOOT

Rnd 1: Knit to double-wrapped st, WW, do not turn; unzip Provisional Cast-On and slip 17 (22) newly live sts to 2nd circular needle (N2) for instep and work Eyelet Rib across new sts, place marker for beg of rnd—35 (45) sts.
Rnd 2: N1: WW, knit to end; N2: work Eyelet Rib across.
Continue in St st (sole) and Eyelet Rib (instep) until 4 (7) total pat reps are complete.

INCREASE FOR GUSSET

Rnd 1: N1: K1, M1R, knit to last st, M1L, K1; N2: work in established pat—37 (47) sts.
Rnd 2: N1: Knit; N2: work in established pat.

Rep Rnds 1 and 2 until there are 30 (41) sts on N1.

HEEL

Row 1 (RS): On N1, k23 (31), W&T.
Row 2: P16, W&T.
Row 3: Knit to st before last wrapped st, W&T.
Row 4: Purl to st before last wrapped st, W&T.
Rep Rows 3 and 4 until 10 (13) sts rem unwrapped in center.
Row 5 (RS): Knit to the first wrapped st, WW, W&T.
Row 6: Purl to the first wrapped st, WW, W&T.
Row 7: Knit to the first double-wrapped st, WW, W&T.
Row 8: Purl to the first double-wrapped st, WW, W&T.
Rep Rows 8 and 9 until all double-wrapped sts are worked.

DECREASE GUSSET

Row 1: Sl 1, knit to 1 st before gap, ssk, turn.
Row 2: Sl 1, purl to 1 st before gap, p2tog, turn.
Rep Rows 1 and 2 until 1 st rem outside gap at each end.

LEG

Rnd 1: N1: Sl 1, knit to 1 st before gap, ssk; N2: work in established Eyelet Rib.
Rnd 2: N1: K2tog, knit to end; N2: work in Eyelet Rib—35 (45) sts with 18 (23) sts on N1 and 17 (22) sts on N2.
Rnd 3: N1: Continue 5-st rep of Eyelet Rib as already established on N2; N2: work in Eyelet Rib.
Work even in Eyelet Rib all around until leg measures 2 inches, ending on Rnd 4.

CUFF

Rnd 1: K2tog, *p1, k1; rep from * around—34 (44) sts.
Rnds 2–10: *K1, p1; rep from * around.
Bind off all sts loosely in rib.

FINISHING

Weave in loose ends. Block as desired. ✪

Daisy Rib Buttoned Leg Warmers

Make a statement on your chilly morning walk in these buttoned leg warmers.

DESIGN BY SARAH WILSON

 EASY

SIZE
One size fits most

FINISHED MEASUREMENTS
12½ inches x 18 inches, unstretched

MATERIALS
- Brown Sheep Burly Spun (bulky weight; 100% wool; 130 yds/226g per skein): 2 skeins prairie fire #BS181
- Size 13 (9mm) needles or size needed to obtain gauge
- Sewing thread to match yarn
- 8 [1-inch] buttons

GAUGE
13 sts and 14 rows= 4 inches/10cm in P1, K1 Rib.
To save time, take time to check gauge.

PATTERN STITCHES
P1, K1 Rib (multiple of 2 sts + 1)
Row 1 (WS): *K1, p1; rep from * to last st, k1.
Row 2 (RS): *P1, k1; rep from * to last st, p1.
  Rep Rows 1 and 2 for pat.
Daisy Rib (multiple of 4 sts + 1)
Row 1 (RS): *P1, k3; rep from * to last st, k1.
Row 2: *K1, p3tog but do not remove from needle, yo, p3tog again, remove from needle; rep from * to last st, k1.
  Rep Rows 1 and 2 for pat.

LEG WARMERS
Cast on 41 sts.
Row 1 (WS): Sl 1, p3, work P1, K1 Rib to last 4 sts, p4.
Row 2 (RS): Sl 1, k3, work P1, K1 Rib to

last 4 sts, k4.

Row 3: Rep Row 1.

Buttonhole row: Sl 1, k2tog, yo, k1, work in established pat across row.

Maintaining edge sts in St st and center sts in P1, K1 Rib, work even for 9 rows.

Next row (RS): Sl 1, k3, work in Daisy Rib to last 4 sts, k4.

Maintaining edge sts in St st and center sts in Daisy Rib, work even for 5 rows.

Work Buttonhole row.

Work even for 15 rows.

Work Buttonhole row.

Work even for 6 rows.

Change to P1, K1 Rib for center sts and work 9 rows.

Work Buttonhole Row.

Work even for 3 rows.

Bind off in pat.

FINISHING

Weave in all ends. Block as desired. Sew buttons opposite buttonholes. ✪

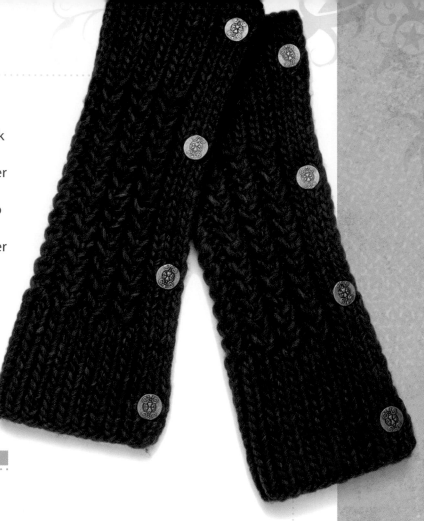

Cozy Cabled Leg Warmers

Look ultra cool, while staying extra warm in this fashion-forward cabled design.

DESIGN BY LAURA NELKIN

 EASY

SIZE
Adult medium

FINISHED MEASUREMENTS
Circumference: Approx 10 inches
Length: 18 inches

MATERIALS
- Schaefer Yarn Esperanza (bulky weight; 70% lambswool/30% alpaca; 280 yds/8 oz per hank): 1 hank Elena Piscopia
- Size 10½ (6.5mm) double-pointed needles (set of 5) or size needed to obtain gauge
- Stitch marker
- Cable needle

GAUGE

15 sts and 20 rnds = 4 inches/10cm in St st. To save time, take time to check gauge.

SPECIAL ABBREVIATION

Cable 6 Forward (C6F): Sl 3 sts to cn and hold in front, k3, k3 from cn.

PATTERN STITCHES

P2, K2 Rib (multiple of 4 sts)
Rnd 1: *P2, k2; rep from* around.
    Rep Rnd 1 for pat.

Cable Panel (10-st panel)
Rnds 1 and 3: P2, k6, p2.
Rnd 2: P2, C6F, p2.
Rnds 4–6: P2, k2, p2, k2, p2.
    Rep Rnds 1–6 for pat.

PATTERN NOTE

For larger sizes, cast on 4 more stitches for every extra inch needed, then work as in pattern.

LEG WARMERS

Cast on 40 sts. Distribute evenly on 4 dpns; place marker for beg of rnd and join, taking care not to twist sts.
    Work 7 rnds in P2, K2 Rib.
Next rnd: Work Cable Panel over 10 sts, knit to end of rnd.
    Work even in established pat until piece measures approx 16½ inches or desired length.
    Work 7 rnds in P2, K2 Rib.
    Bind off loosely in pat.

FINISHING

Weave in ends. Block lightly. ✪

If you're looking for the perfect gift, you've come to the right place. We've assembled some enticing hat and sock ensembles on the pages that follow.

SETS

If you need to please that man in your life, we've got some sporty striped sock and hat combinations to suit his style. Don't forget the colorful caps and booties for babies and socks for kids, too!

Three Times a Delight

Just like the saying goes— everything good comes in threes!

DESIGNS BY AMY MARSHALL

◖◼◼◻ INTERMEDIATE

SIZES

Infant's small (medium, large) to fit newborn (3–12, 12–24) months Instructions are given for smallest size, with larger sizes in parentheses. When only 1 number is given, it applies to all sizes.

FINISHED MEASUREMENTS

Hat circumference: 15 (17, 18) inches
Booties ribbed cuff length: Approx 4¾ (5, 5¼) inches
Booties rolled cuff length: Approx 3¾ (4, 4¼) inches
Foot length: Approx 2½ (3½, 4½) inches

MATERIALS

- Filatura di Crosa Zara (DK weight; 100% merino wool; 137 yds/50g per ball): 1 ball each oatmeal #1451 (MC) and off-white #1396 (A) for each set and 1 ball each of B and C as follows: Heart set—true blue #1754 (B), light blue #1462 (C); Flower set—petunia #1723 (B), cotton candy #1510 (C); Star set—kelly green #1727 (B), sage green #18 (C)
- Size 6 (4mm) straight and double-pointed needles (set of 4) or size needed to obtain gauge
- Size F/5 (3.75mm) crochet hook
- Stitch markers, 1 in CC for beg of rnd
- Bobbins (optional)

GAUGE

20 sts and 28 rows = 4 inches/10cm in St st.
To save time, take time to check gauge.

SPECIAL ABBREVIATIONS

Make 1 Left (M1L): Insert LH needle from front to back under the running thread between the last st worked and next st on LH needle. With RH needle, knit (or purl) into the back of this loop.
Make 1 Right (M1R): Insert LH needle from back to front under the running thread between the last st worked and next st on LH needle. With RH needle, knit (or purl) into the front of this loop.
N1, N2, N3: Needle 1, Needle 2, Needle 3

PATTERN NOTES

The socks are worked from the cuff down (with 2 options given for cuff), then the instep is worked following chart (3 options given), after which stitches are picked up all around to work the sole.

The charts are worked using intarsia method (page 164); on hat, extend stripe pattern behind heart/flower/star across entire width of the hat.

Work color areas using bobbins or lengths of yarn; cut lengths of yarn for each color area allowing ¾ inch for each stitch plus 10 inches total for tails on both ends.

ending with a WS row.

Cut B and C and leave sts on needle.

With MC, cast on 10 (11, 11) sts, knit across 14 (17, 20) sts of first ear flap, cast on 24 (28, 28) sts, knit across 14 (17, 20) sts of second ear flap, cast on 10 (11, 11) sts—72 (84, 90) sts.

Work in St st until piece measures approx ½ inch from ear flaps, ending with a WS row.

Extending stripe pat across entire width of hat and centering motif, work Chart A of desired motif.

Work even in MC until piece measures approx 3¾ (3¾, 4¼) inches from ear flaps, ending with a WS row.

CROWN

Dec row (RS): *K10 (12, 13), k2tog; rep from *, ending k9 (11, 12), k2tog, k1— 66 (78, 84) sts.

Continue to dec 6 sts [every RS row] 7 (9, 12) more times, knitting 1 st fewer between each dec on each succeeding dec row—24 (24, 12) sts.

Next row (WS): P1 (1, 0), p2tog, p1 (1, 0), *p2tog, p2 (2, 0), rep from * across— 18 (18, 6) sts.

Small and Medium only

Next row: Work Dec row as established—12 sts.

Next row: P2tog across—6 sts.

Cut yarn, leaving a 6-inch tail.

With tapestry needle, thread tail through rem and pull tight. Secure end.

FINISHING

Sew center back seam using mattress st and ½-st seam allowance, being careful to match stripes.

With RS facing and beg at center back, using crochet hook and B, work sc to beg of ear flap, around ear flap, across front brim, around 2nd ear flap, and back to center back; join with slip st. Work 1 rnd

Hat

EAR FLAPS

Make 2

With straight needles and C, cast on 4 (3, 4) sts.

Row 1 (RS): Knit.

Row 2: P1, M1L, purl to last st, M1R, p1.

Row 3: With B, k1, M1R, knit to last st, M1L, k1.

Row 4: With B, rep Row 2—one stripe sequence complete.

Continue alternating 2 rows C, 2 rows B and inc at each edge [every row] twice more, then [every RS row] 0 (2, 3) times—14 (17, 20) sts.

Continue in stripe sequence until piece measures 2½ (3, 3½) inches from beg,

of rev sc in each st just worked; join with slip st and fasten off. Weave in all ends.

Booties

RIBBED CUFF (OPTION 1)

With B, cast on 24 (30, 34) sts. Distribute sts on 3 dpns as follows: N1: 6 (8, 9) sts, N2: 11 (13, 15) sts, N3: 7 (9, 10) sts. Place marker for beg of rnd and join, being careful not to twist sts.

Work in K1, P1 Rib for 2 rnds.

Change to MC and work in K1, P1 Rib until piece measures approx 2¾ inches from beg.

Next rnd (inc): K2, M1L, knit to end—25 (31, 35) sts.

Continue to work in St st until piece measures approx 3 inches from beg. Cut MC.

Continue with Instep instructions.

ROLLED CUFF (OPTION 2)

With B, cast on 25 (31, 35) sts. Distribute sts on 3 dpns as follows: N1: 7 (9, 10) sts, N2: 11 (13, 15) sts, N3: 7 (9, 10) sts. Place marker for beg of rnd and join, being careful not to twist sts.

Work 2 rnds in St st.

Change to MC and work in St st until piece measures approx 2 inches from beg. Cut MC.

Continue with Instep instructions.

INSTEP

Working on N2 only, reattach yarn and work Chart B for desired motif, beg and end where indicated on chart for size being worked.

Weave in ends on instep before working sole.

SOLE

Rnd 1: N1: With B, knit across, then, pick up and knit 7 (9, 12) sts along side of instep; N2: knit; N3: pick up and knit 7 (9, 11) sts along 2nd side of instep, knit to end. Place marker for beg of rnd and join—39 (49, 59) sts.

Rnd 2: With B, knit.

Rnds 3 and 4: With C, knit. (1 stripe sequence completed)

Continue in stripe pat as established, alternating 2 rnds B, 2 rnds C, until sole measures approx 1¼ (1½, 1¾) inches.

Next rnd: K18 (23, 28), place marker, k3, place marker, knit to end.

Dec rnd: K1, ssk, knit to 2 sts before marker, k2tog, slip marker, k3, slip marker, ssk, knit to last 3 sts, k2tog, k1—35 (45, 55) sts.

Rep [Dec rnd] twice—27 (37, 47) sts.

Divide 5 (7, 9) sts rem on N2 and slip to N1 and N3.

Weave center edges of sole tog using Kitchener st (page 17).

FINISHING

Weave in all ends. Block as necessary. ✪

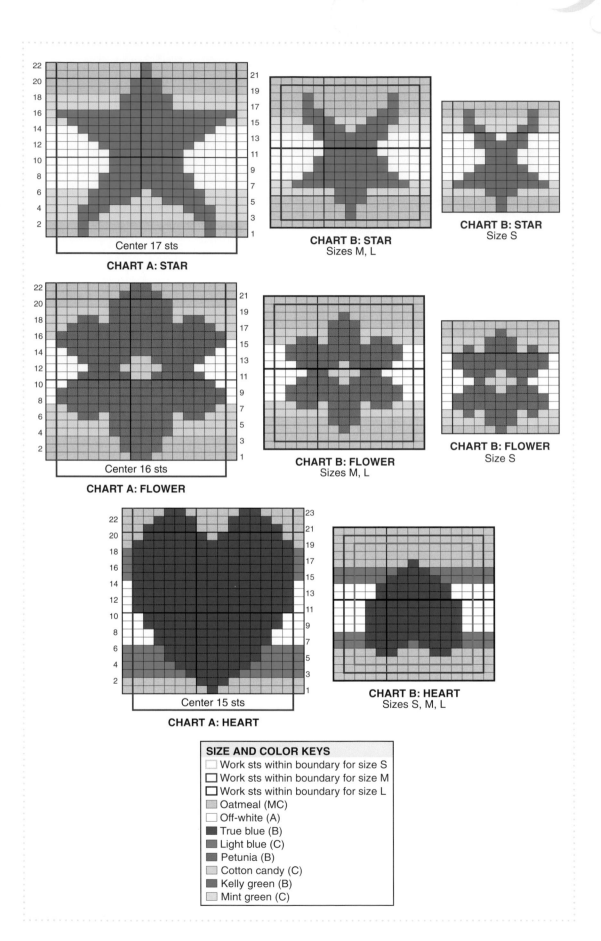

Center 17 sts

CHART A: STAR

CHART B: STAR
Sizes M, L

CHART B: STAR
Size S

Center 16 sts

CHART A: FLOWER

CHART B: FLOWER
Sizes M, L

CHART B: FLOWER
Size S

Center 15 sts

CHART A: HEART

CHART B: HEART
Sizes S, M, L

SIZE AND COLOR KEYS
☐ Work sts within boundary for size S
☐ Work sts within boundary for size M
☐ Work sts within boundary for size L
▨ Oatmeal (MC)
☐ Off-white (A)
■ True blue (B)
▨ Light blue (C)
▨ Petunia (B)
▨ Cotton candy (C)
▨ Kelly green (B)
▨ Mint green (C)

Wee Baby Bamboozle Hat & Socks

This multi-colored hat and socks set will be a bright and cheery outfit for Baby to wear.

DESIGNS BY LAURA ANDERSSON

▰▰▰▱ INTERMEDIATE

SIZES

Socks: Newborn (3–6, 6–9, 9–12, 12–18) months

Hat: 0–6 (6–18) months Instructions are given for smallest size, with larger size(s) in parentheses. When only 1 number is given, it applies to all sizes.

FINISHED MEASUREMENTS

Sock Circumference: 3¾ (3¾, 4¼, 5, 5¾) inches

Foot length: 3½ (3½, 4, 4, 4½) inches

Hat Circumference: 14½ (16) inches

MATERIALS

- Crystal Palace Bamboozle (worsted weight; 55% bamboo/24% cotton/21% elastic nylon; 90 yds/50g per ball): 1 ball each yellow #3646 (MC), fern #9806 (A), sprite green #2342 (B), and limeade #1240 (C) **[4 MEDIUM]**
- Size 4 (3.5mm) double-pointed (set of 4) and 16-inch circular needles or size needed to obtain gauge
- Stitch markers, 1 in CC for beg of rnd

GAUGE

22 sts and 36 rnds = 4 inches/10cm in St st and stranded St st.

To save time, take time to check gauge.

SPECIAL ABBREVIATIONS

N1, N2, N3: Needle 1, Needle 2, Needle 3

PATTERN NOTES

The sock is worked on 3 double-pointed needles from the cuff down, with a heel flap, gusset and wedge toe.

Work 2 gauge swatches and if necessary, go up in needle size for stranded stockinette section.

For hat, change to double-pointed needles when stitches no longer fit comfortably on circular needle.

Socks

CUFF

With MC and dpn, cast on 20 (20, 24, 28, 32) sts. Do not join.

Purl 1 row, distributing sts on 3 dpns; place marker for beg of rnd and join, taking care not to twist sts.

Rnds 1–4: With MC, work in K2, P2 Rib. Cut MC.

Rnds 5–9: Change to A and continue in established rib.

Rnd 10: Purl around. Cut A.

Rnds 11–15: Change to B; [knit 1 rnd, purl 1 rnd] twice, knit 1 rnd.

Rnds 16 and 17: Join C; *k2 B, k2 C; rep from * around.

Rnds 18 and 19: *K2 C, k2 B; rep from * around. Cut B.

Rnds 20 and 21: With C, purl around.

Rnds 22 and 23: Join A; *k2 A, k2C; rep from * around.

Rnds 24 and 25: *K2 C, k2 A; rep from * around. Cut C.

Rnds 26 and 27: Join MC; *k2 A, k2 MC; rep from * around.

Rnds 28 and 29: *K2 MC, k2 A; rep from * around.

Rnd 30: With A, purl around.

Rnd 31: With MC, purl around.

Rnds 32–34: With A, knit around.

Rnds 35–37: With MC, knit around. Cut MC.

HEEL FLAP

Row 1 (RS): Change to A; k6 (6, 7, 7, 8) sts, turn.

Row 2: P12 (12, 14, 14, 16) for heel; sl rem 8 (8, 10, 14, 16) sts to 1 or 2 dpns for instep.

Row 3: *Sl 1, k1; rep from * across.

Row 4: Sl 1, purl to end of row.

Rep Rows 3 and 4 until the heel measures 1 (1, 1¼, 1¼, 1½) inches.

HEEL TURN

Row 1 (RS): Sl 1, k6 (6, 7, 7, 8), ssk, k1, turn.

Row 2: Sl 1, p3, p2tog, p1, turn.

Row 3: Sl 1, knit to 1 st before gap, ssk, k1, turn.

Row 4: Sl 1, purl to 1 st before gap, p2tog, p1, turn.

Rep Rows 3 and 4 until all sts are used. If necessary, omit the k1 and p1 following dec on last 2 rows—8 (8, 8, 8, 10) sts.

GUSSET

Set-up rnd: With a spare dpn, k4 (4, 4, 4, 5); with N1, k4 (4, 4, 4, 5), then pick up and knit 1 st in each of the slipped sts along the side of flap; with N2, work instep sts in rib as follows: p1 (1, 2, 2, 1), k2, *p2, k2; rep from * to last 1 (1, 2, 2, 1) instep st(s), p1 (1, 2, 2, 1); with N3, pick up and knit 1 st in each of the slipped sts along the side of flap, then knit sts from the spare dpn. Place marker for beg of rnd in center of heel.

Rnd 1: Work even in pat as established. Cut A.

Rnd 2 (dec): Change to B and work as follows: N1: knit to last 3 sts, k2tog, k1; N2: work established rib; N3: k1, ssk, knit to end of rnd.

Work last 2 rnds until 20 (20, 24, 28, 32) sts rem.

FOOT

Work even until foot measures 3 (3, 3½, 3½, 3½) inches. Cut B.

TOE

Rnd 1 (dec): Change to MC; N1: knit to last 3 sts, k2tog, k1; N2: k1, ssk, knit to last 3 sts, k2tog, k1—16 (16, 20, 24, 28) sts.

Rnd 2: Knit around.

Rep [Rnds 1 and 2] 0 (0, 0, 1, 2) times—16 (16, 20, 20, 20) sts.

Rep [Rnd 1] 2 (2, 3, 3, 3) times—8 sts.

Cut yarn, leaving an 8-inch tail.

Using tapestry needle, thread tail through rem sts, and pull tight. Secure on WS.

FINISHING

Weave in all ends. Block.

Hat

CUFF

With circular needle and MC, cast on 80 (88) sts. Do not join.

Purl 1 row, place marker for beg of rnd and join, taking care not to twist sts.

Work 7 rnds in K2, P2 Rib.

Purl 1 rnd. Cut MC.

Change to A and work 9 rnds in rib as established. Cut A.

BODY

Change to B; [knit 1 rnd, purl 1 rnd] twice, knit 1 rnd.

Join MC and work as follows:

Rnds 1–3: *K2 B, k2 MC; rep from * around.

Rnds 4–6: *K2 MC, k2 B; rep from* around.

Rnds 7–9: Rep Rnds 1–3. Cut B.

With MC, purl 1 rnd.

Join C and work as follows:

Rnds 1–3: *K2 MC, k2 C; rep from * around.

Rnds 4–6: *K2 C, k2 MC; rep from * around.

With C, purl 1 rnd. Cut C.

Join A and work as follows:

Rnds 1–3: *K2 MC, k2 A; rep from * around.

Rnds 4–6: *K2 A, k2 MC; rep from * around.

Purl 1 rnd A, placing markers every 10 (11) sts.

CROWN

Larger Size Only

Dec rnd: With MC, *k1, purl to 3 sts from marker, k1, k2tog; rep from * around—80 sts.

Work 1 rnd even in established pat. Cut MC.

Both Sizes

Dec rnd: With A, *k1, purl to 3 sts from marker, k1, k2tog; rep from * around—72 sts.

Next rnd: Work even in established pat.

Rep [last 2 rnds] 3 times, then work Dec rnd once more; cut A—40 sts.

With B, work [Dec rnd] twice; cut B and remove markers—24 sts.

Next rnd: With MC, *k1, p2tog; rep from * around—16 sts.

Next 2 rnds: P2tog around—4 sts.

Bind off pwise.

FINISHING

Weave in all ends. Block. ✪

Walking Spiral Hat & Socks

This combo will keep your young ones toasty and looking as cute as ever!

DESIGNS BY LAURA NELKIN

▬▬▬▭ INTERMEDIATE

SIZES
Infant's small (medium, large) to fit 0–6 (6–18, 18–36) months Instructions are given for smallest size, with larger sizes in parentheses. When only 1 number is given, it applies to all sizes.

FINISHED MEASUREMENTS
Sock circumference: 4½ (5, 5½) inches
Hat circumference: 13½ (15, 16¾) inches (unstretched)

MATERIALS
- Schaefer Yarn Lola (DK weight; 100% merino wool superwash; 280 yds/4 oz per skein): 1 skein Hermione

  3 LIGHT
- Size 2 (2.75mm) double-pointed needles (set of 5) or size needed to obtain gauge (socks)
- Size 4 (3.5mm) double-pointed needles (set of 5) or size needed to obtain gauge (hat)
- Stitch marker

GAUGE
Hat: 24 sts and 32 rnds = 4 inches/10cm in pat.
Socks: 26 sts and 36 rnds = 4 inches/10cm in St st.
To save time, take time to check gauge.

SPECIAL ABBREVIATIONS
Knit in Front and Back (kfb): Knit in front and back loops of st.
Make 1 Left (M1L): Insert LH needle from front to back under the running thread between the last st worked and next st on LH needle. With RH needle, knit into the back of this loop.
Make 1 Right (M1R): Insert LH needle from back to front under the running thread between the last st worked and next st on LH needle. With RH needle, knit into the front of this loop.
N1, N2, N3, N4: Needle 1, Needle 2, Needle 3, Needle 4

PATTERN STITCHES
Spiral Rib (Hat) (multiple of 10 sts)
Rnd 1: *P1, k4, p2, k3; rep from * around.
Rnd 2: *K1, p1, k4, p2, k2; rep from * around.
Rnd 3: *K2, p1, k4, p2, k1; rep from * around.
Rnd 4: *K3, p1, k4, p2; rep from * around.
Rnd 5: *P1, k3, p1, k4, p1; rep from * around.
Rnd 6: *P2, k3, p1, k4; rep from * around.
Rnd 7: *K1, p2, k3, p1, k3; rep from * around.
Rnd 8: *K2, p2, k3, p1, k2; rep from * around.
Rnd 9: *K3, p2, k3, p1, k1; rep from * around.
Rnd 10: *K4, p2, k3, p1; rep from * around.
   Rep Rnds 1–10 for pat.

Spiral Rib (Sock) (multiple of 14 [16, 18] sts)

Rnd 1: *K4 (4, 5), p2, k3 (3, 4), p1, k2 (4, 4), p2; rep from * around.

Rnd 2: *P1, k4 (4, 5), p2, k3 (3, 4), p1, k2 (4, 4), p1; rep from * around.

Rnd 3: *P2, k4 (4, 5), p2, k3 (3, 4), p1, k2 (4, 4); rep from * around.

Rnd 4: *K1, p2, k4 (4, 5), p2, k3 (3, 4), p1, k1 (3, 3); rep from * around.

Continue working pat in this manner, moving purl sts 1 st over each rnd.

SPECIAL TECHNIQUE

I-Cord: *K3, do not turn, slip sts back to LH needle; rep from * until cord is desired length. Bind off.

PATTERN NOTE

The socks are worked on 3 double-pointed needles from the cuff down with a heel flap, gusset and "star" toe.

Hat

FIRST EARFLAP

Cast on 2 (2, 3) sts.
   Purl 1 row.

Small and Medium only
Next row: Kfb twice—4 sts.
Next row: Purl.

All Sizes
Work Rows 1–14 (1–14, 1–20) of Earflap

chart for size you are making.
   Cut yarn, leaving a 6-inch tail. Set aside.

2ND EARFLAP

Work as for first earflap, but work through Row 15 (15, 21) of chart.
   Do not cut yarn.

JOIN EARFLAPS

Using backward loop method, cast on 20 (20, 25) sts, work Row 15 (15, 21) of Earflap chart across first earflap, cast on 20 (20, 25) sts; place marker for beg of rnd and join, taking care not to twist sts—80 (90, 100) sts.

BODY

Continue working in established Spiral Rib pat (moving purl sts over 1 st on each succeeding rnd) for 40 (50, 60) rnds, ending with Rnd 10.

CROWN

Work Crown Decrease Chart; chart rep will be worked 8 (9, 10) times around—4 (5, 5) sts rem when chart is complete.
Last rnd: K2tog, k1 (k2tog, k2tog), k1—3 sts.
   Work I-cord on rem 3 sts for 3 inches.
   Bind off.
   Tie I-cord into a knot.

FINISHING

Weave in all ends. Block as necessary.

Socks

CUFF AND LEG

Cast on 28 (32, 36) sts; distribute sts to 3 dpns as follows: N1: 14 (16, 18) sts; N2 and N3: 7 (8, 9) sts each. Place marker for beg of rnd and join, taking care not to twist sts.
   Work K1, P1 Rib for 4 (5, 7) rnds.
   Work Spiral Rib (Sock) until piece measures 1½ (2½, 3) inches from beg.

HEEL FLAP

Work back and forth on N1 (heel sts), with

sts on N2 and N3 on hold for instep.

Row 1 (RS): *Sl 1, k1; rep from * to end of row.

Row 2: Sl 1, purl to end.

Rep [Rows 1 and 2] 6 (7, 8) times—7 (8, 9) chain sts at each edge.

TURN HEEL

Row 1 (RS): K9 (10, 11), ssk, k1, turn work.

Row 2: (WS): Sl 1, p5, p2tog, p1, turn.

Row 3: Sl 1, knit to 1 st before gap, ssk (1 st from each side of gap), k1, turn.

Row 4: Sl 1, purl to 1 st before gap, p2tog (1 st from each side of gap), p1, turn.

Rep Rows 3 and 4 until all heel sts have been worked, ending with a WS row—10 (10, 12) heel sts rem.

SHAPE GUSSETS

Rnd 1: N1: K10 (10, 12) heel sts, then pick up and knit 7 (8, 9) sts along edge of heel flap, M1 in running thread between heel and instep sts; N2: knit across 14 (16, 18) instep sts; N3: M1 in running thread between instep and heel sts, pick up and knit 7 (8, 9) sts along other edge of heel flap, then k5 (5, 6) from N1, place marker for beg of rnd—40 (44, 50) sts distributed as follows: N1 and N3: 13 (14, 16) sts each (sole); N2: 14 (16, 18) sts (instep).

Rnd 2: N1: Knit to last 3 sts, k2tog, k1; N2: knit; N3: k1, ssk, knit to end—38 (42, 48) sts.

Rnd 3: Knit around.

Rep Rnds 2 and 3 until 28 (32, 36) sts rem.

FOOT

Work even in St st until piece measures 3 (4, 5) inches from back of heel, or approx 1 inch less than desired total foot length.

TOE

Redistribute sts evenly onto 4 needles.

Rnd 1: N1: Knit to last 2 sts, k2tog; rep on N2, N3 and N4—24 (28, 32) sts.

Rep Rnd 1 until 4 sts rem.

Cut yarn, leaving a 5-inch tail. Using tapestry needle, thread tail through rem sts, and pull tight; secure to WS.

FINISHING

Weave in all ends. Block as necessary. ✪

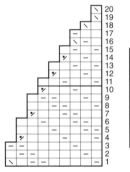

STITCH KEY
- ☐ K on RS, p on WS
- ⊟ P on RS, k on WS
- ML M1L
- MR M1R
- ◲ Ssk
- ◳ P2tog

CROWN DEC CHART

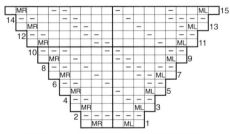

EARFLAP CHART (SMALL/MEDIUM)

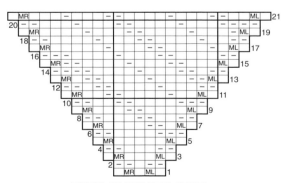

EARFLAP CHART (LARGE)

Orange You My Baby

This scalloped-edge brimmed hat with matching socks will stand out in the crowd!

DESIGNS BY LAURA ANDERSSON

 EASY

SIZES
Hat: Infant's 0–9 (9–18) months
Socks: Infant's 0–6 (6–9, 9–12, 12–18) months. Instructions are given for the smallest size, with larger sizes in parentheses. When only 1 number is given, it applies to all sizes.

FINISHED MEASUREMENTS
Hat circumference (unstretched): 15 (16) inches
Sock circumference (unstretched): 3 (4, 4, 4) inches
Sock length (foot): 4 (4¼, 4¾, 5¼) inches

MATERIALS
- Crystal Palace Panda Silk (fingering weight; 52% bamboo/43% superwash merino wool/ 5% combed silk; 204 yds/50g per ball): 1 (1, 2, 2) balls persimmon tones #4004
- Size 3 (3.25mm) double-pointed (set of 4) and 16-inch circular needles or size needed to obtain gauge (hat)
- Size 2 (2.75mm) double-pointed needles (set of 4) or size needed to obtain gauge (socks)
- Stitch markers, 1 in CC for beg of rnd

GAUGE
Hat: 40 sts and 40 rnds = 4 inches/10cm in K2, P2 Rib (unstretched) with larger needles.
Socks: 48 sts and 44 rnds = 4 inches/10cm in K2, P2 Rib (unstretched) with smaller needles.
To save time, take time to check gauge.

SPECIAL ABBREVIATIONS
N1, N2, N3: Needle 1, Needle 2, Needle 3
Make 1 (M1): Insert LH needle from front to back under the running thread between the last st worked and next st on LH needle. With RH needle, knit into the back of this loop.

PATTERN STITCH
Scallop Pat (multiple of 12 sts)
Rnd 1: *[K2tog] twice, [yo, k1] 3 times, yo, [ssk] twice, k1; rep from * around.
Rnd 2: Knit.
Rnd 3: Purl.
Rnd 4: Knit.
Rnds 5–8: Rep Rnds 1–4.
Rnd 9: *[K2tog] twice, [M1, k1] 3 times, M1, [ssk] twice, k1; rep from * around.
Rnd 10: Knit.
Rnd 11: Purl.
Rnd 12: Knit.
Rnds 13–16: Rep Rnds 9–12.

SPECIAL TECHNIQUE
Knitted cast on: Make slip knot and put on LH needle. Insert RH needle into knot from front to back and *wrap yarn around needle as if to knit. Insert LH needle tip from front to back into resulting st, keeping both needles in st. Rep from

* until all sts are cast on, then remove RH needle. **Note:** *Sts accumulate on LH needle.*

When working hat, change to double-pointed needles when stitches no longer fit comfortably on circular needle.

Socks are knit on 3 double-pointed needles from the cuff down with a heel flap and gusset and wedge toe.

Hat

EDGING

With larger circular needle and using Knitted Cast-On, cast on 196 (224) sts; place marker for beg of rnd and join, taking care not to twist sts.
Rnd 1: Purl.
Rnd 2: *K2, slip last st back to LH needle, pass 4 sts over this st, then slip the st to RH needle, k1; rep from * around—84 (96) sts.
   Knit 2 rnds.
   Work 16 rnds of Scallop Pat.

BODY

Work in K2, P2 Rib for 2 (2½) inches.
   Purl 2 rnds.
   Work in P2, K2 Rib for 1 (1½) inches.
Next rnd: *P12, place marker; rep from * around.

CROWN

Dec rnd: *P1, knit to 3 sts before marker, p1, p2tog; rep from * around—77 (88) sts.
Next rnd: *P1, knit to 2 sts before marker, p2; rep from * around.
   Rep [last 2 rnds] 7 times, removing markers on last rnd—28 (32) sts.
Next rnd: *K2, k2tog; rep from * around—21 (24) sts.
Next rnd: *K1, k2tog; rep from * around—14 (16) sts.
Next rnd: K2tog around—7 (8) sts.

Cut yarn, leaving a 5-inch tail.
   Using tapestry needle, thread tail through rem sts, and pull tight and secure on WS.

FINISHING

Weave in all ends. Wash and lay flat to dry without stretching.

Socks

EDGING

With smaller dpns, cast on 91 (112, 112, 119) sts; place marker for beg of rnd and join, taking care not to twist sts.
Rnd 1: Purl.
Rnd 2: *K2, place the last st knit back onto LH needle; pass 4 sts over, k2; rep from * around—39 (48, 48, 51) sts.

CUFF

Knit and dec 3 (0, 0, 3) sts evenly around—36 (48, 48, 48) sts.
   Purl 1 rnd.
   Work 16 rnds of Scallop Pat.
   Knit 1 rnd, purl 2 rnds.

TURN CUFF

At the marker, M1 and place onto LH needle. Remove marker and turn the sock inside out. The M1 is now on RH needle, and you will work it tog with the last st in the rnd.

LEG

Work in P2, K2 Rib for 2¼ (2¼, 2½, 2½) inches.
   Purl 1 rnd.
   Work in K2, P2 rib for ¾ (¾, 1, 1) inch.

HEEL

Row 1 (RS): K10 (13, 13, 13), turn.
Row 2: Sl 1, p19 (25, 25, 25) sts, turn, leaving rem 16 (22, 22, 22) sts on hold on dpn for instep.
Row 3: *Sl 1, k1; rep from * to end.
Row 4: Sl 1, purl to end.

Rep Rows 3 and 4 until heel measures 1¼ (1½, 1¾, 2) inches.

HEEL TURN

Row 1 (RS): K11 (14, 14, 14), ssk, k1, turn.
Row 2: Sl 1, p3, p2tog, p1, turn.
Row 3: Sl 1, knit to 1 st before gap, ssk, k1, turn.
Row 4: Sl 1, purl to 1 st before gap, p2tog, p1, turn.

Rep Rows 3 and 4 until all sts have been worked, ending with a WS row. (**Note:** *On larger sizes, do not work k1 (p1) following dec on last 2 rows*)—12 (14, 14, 14) sts rem.

GUSSET

Set-up rnd: With a spare dpn, sl 1, k5 (5, 6); with N1, k6 (7, 7, 7), then pick up and knit 1 st in each slip st along left side of flap; with N2, work across 16 (22, 22, 22) instep sts as follows: k1 (2, 2, 2), *p2, k2; rep from * to last 3 (0, 0, 0) sts, p2 (0, 0, 0), k1 (0, 0, 0); with N3, pick up and knit 1 st in each slip st along right side of flap, then k6 (7, 7, 7) sts from spare dpn. Place marker for beg of rnd in center of heel.
Rnd 1: Work even in established pat.
Rnd 2 (dec): N1: Knit to last 3 sts, k2tog, k1; N2: work even in established rib; N3: k1, ssk, knit to end.

Rep Rnds 1 and 2 until 36 (48, 48, 48) sts rem.

FOOT

Work even until foot measures approx 3 (4¼, 3½, 4) inches.

TOE

Dec Rnd: N1: Knit to last 3 sts, k2tog, k1; N2: k1, ssk, knit to last 3 sts, k2tog, k1; N3: k1, ssk, knit to end—32 (44, 44, 44) sts.
Next rnd: Work even.

Rep [last 2 rnds] 3 (6) times—20 sts.

Rep Dec rnd 3 times—8 sts.

Cut yarn, leaving an 8-inch tail; using tapestry needle, thread tail through rem sts, pull tight and secure on WS.

FINISHING

Weave in all ends. Wash and lay flat to dry without stretching. ✪

Simple Self-Striping Skullcap & Socks

Complement any outfit with this casual combo.

DESIGNS BY ELLEN EDWARDS DRECHSLER (HAT)
AND KATE ATHERLEY (SOCKS)

■■■□ INTERMEDIATE

SIZES

Hat: Adult's average
Socks: Woman's small (woman's large, man's small, man's large) to fit woman's shoe sizes 5–7 (7½–9) and man's shoe sizes 6–9 (9½–11) Instructions are given for smallest size, with larger sizes in parentheses. When only 1 number is given, it applies to all sizes.

FINISHED MEASUREMENTS

Hat circumference: 22 inches
Sock circumference: 7½ (8, 8½, 9) inches
Foot length: 9 (10, 10, 11) inches

MATERIALS

- Premier Yarns Echo (sock weight; 68% superwash wool/22% polyamide/10% cotton; 186 yds/50g per ball): 1 ball dark pinks/light blues #42-205 for hat and 2 balls dark pinks/light blues #42-205 for socks
- Size 1 (2.25 mm) double-pointed needles (set of 4) or size needed to obtain gauge (socks)
- Size 3 (3.25mm) double-pointed and 16-inch circular needles or size needed to obtain gauge (hat)
- Stitch markers, 1 in CC for beg of rnd

1 SUPER FINE

GAUGE

Hat: 26 sts and 32 rnds = 4 inches/10cm in St st with larger needles.
Socks: 30 sts and 42 rnds = 4 inches/10cm in St st with smaller needles. To save time, take time to check gauge.

SPECIAL ABBREVIATIONS

N1, N2, N3: Needle 1, needle 2, needle 3

PATTERN NOTES

When working hat, change to double-pointed needles when stitches no longer fit comfortably on circular needle.

This sock is worked on 3 double-pointed needles from the cuff down, with a heel flap, gusset and a wedge toe.

Hat

BRIM

Cast on 140 sts; place marker for beg of rnd and join, taking care not to twist sts.
Work K2, P2 Rib for 1 inch.

BODY

Change to St st and work even until piece measures 6 inches.
Next rnd: *K17, place marker, k16, k2tog, place marker; rep from * around—136 sts. Work 1 rnd even.
Dec rnd: *Knit to 2 sts before marker, k2tog; rep from * around—128 sts.
Rep Dec rnd every other rnd until 8 sts rem.

Remove markers and cut yarn, leaving an 8-inch tail. Using tapestry needle, thread tail through rem sts, pull tight and secure to WS.

Weave in all ends. Block.

Socks

Cast on 56 (60, 64, 68) sts. Distribute evenly on 3 dpns; place marker for beg of rnd and join, taking care not to twist sts.

Work K2, P2 Rib for 2 inches.

Change to St st and work even until leg measures 6 (6½, 7½, 8) inches.

Row 1 (RS): K14 (15, 15, 17), turn.

Row 2: P28 (30, 32, 34), turn, leaving rem 28 (30, 32, 34) sts on hold on dpns for instep.

Row 3: Sl 1, knit across heel sts.

Row 4: Sl 1, purl across heel sts.

Rep [Rows 3 and 4] 8 (9, 10, 11) times.

TURN HEEL

Row 1 (RS): Sl 1, k18 (19, 20, 22), ssk, turn.
Row 2: Sl 1, p10 (10, 10, 12), p2tog, turn.
Row 3: Sl 1, k10 (10, 10, 12), ssk, turn.

Rep Rows 2 and 3 until all sts have been worked, ending with a WS row—12 (12, 12, 14) sts.

GUSSET

Set-up rnd: With N1, sl 1, knit across heel sts, then pick up and knit 14 (15, 16, 17) sts along left side of flap; with N2, knit across instep sts; with N3, pick up and knit 14 (15, 16, 17) sts along right side of flap, then k6 (6, 6, 7) sts from N1. Place marker for beg of rnd in center of heel—68 (72, 76, 82) sts distributed as follows: 20 (21, 22, 24) sts on both N1 and N3; 28 (30, 32, 34) sts on N2.
Rnd 1: Knit around, knitting into back loop of all picked-up sts.
Rnd 2 (dec): N1: Knit to last 3 sts, k2tog, k1; N2: knit across; N3: k1, ssk, knit to end.

Rnd 3: Knit around.

Rep Rnds 2 and 3 until 56 (60, 64, 68) sts rem with 14 (15, 16, 17) sts on N1 and N3.

FOOT

Work even until foot measures 7 (8, 8, 9) inches or approx 2 inches short of desired length.

TOE

Dec rnd: *N1: Knit to last 3 sts, k2tog, k1; N2: k1, ssk, knit to last 3 sts, k2tog, k1; N3: k1, ssk, knit to end—52 (56, 60, 64) sts.

Rep Dec rnd [every 4 rnds] once, [every 3 rnds] twice, [every other rnd] 3 times, then every rnd until 8 sts rem.

Cut yarn, leaving a 6-inch tail.

Using tapestry needle, thread tail through rem sts, and pull tight and secure on WS.

FINISHING

Weave in all ends. Block. ✪

Man's Racing Stripe Cap & Socks

He'll be looking sharp in stripes wearing this cap and matching socks.

DESIGNS BY ERSSIE MAJOR

◼◼◼◻ INTERMEDIATE

SIZES

Cap: Man's average
Socks: Man's small (large) to fit shoe sizes 6–10 (11–14) Instructions are given for smaller size, with larger size in parentheses. When only 1 number is given, it applies to both sizes.

FINISHED MEASUREMENTS

Cap circumference: 18 inches (unstretched)
Sock circumference: 9 (10) inches
Foot length: 10 (11) inches

MATERIALS

- Sublime Cashmere Merino Silk Aran (worsted weight; 75% extra fine merino/20% silk/5% cashmere; 94 yds/50g per ball): 2 balls clipper #15 (MC); 1 ball granite #18 (for hat)
- Austermann Step Sock Yarn (sock weight; 75% superwash virgin wool/25% nylon with jojoba and aloe vera; 459 yds/100g per ball): 1 ball ocean #29 (for sock, if making size large with longer leg/foot, an extra ball may be needed)
- Size 8 (5mm) double-pointed needles (set of 5) and 16-inch circular needle or size to obtain gauge (hat)
- Size 2 (2.75mm) double-pointed needles (set of 5) or size to needed to obtain gauge (socks)
- Size D/3 (3.25mm) crochet hook
- Stitch markers, 1 in CC for beg of rnd

GAUGE

Hat: 18 sts and 24 rnds = 4 inches/10cm in St st.
Socks: 30 sts and 42 rnds = 4 inches/10cm in St st.
To save time, take time to check gauge.

SPECIAL ABBREVIATIONS

Wrap and Turn (W&T): Bring yarn to RS of work between needles, slip next st pwise to RH needle, bring yarn around this st to WS, slip st back to LH needle, turn work to begin working back in the other direction.

Work wrapped sts and wraps tog (WW): *On RS:* Knit to wrapped st, slip the wrapped st pwise from LH needle to RH needle. Use tip of LH needle to pick up wrap(s) and place it/them on RH needle. Slip wrap(s) and st back to LH needle and knit them tog.

On WS: Purl to wrapped st, slip the wrapped st kwise from LH needle to RH needle. Use tip of LH to pick up wrap(s) and place it/them on RH needle. Slip wrap(s) and st back to LH needle and purl them tog.

N1, N2, N3, N4: Needle 1, Needle 2, Needle 3, Needle 4

Make 1 (M1): Insert LH needle from front to back under the running thread between the last st worked and next st on LH needle. With RH needle, knit into the back of this loop.

PATTERN STITCH

Wide Rib (multiple of 6 sts)
Rnd 1: *K4, p2; rep from * around.
 Rep Rnd 1 for pat.

SPECIAL TECHNIQUE

Provisional Cast On: With crochet hook and waste yarn, make a chain several sts longer than desired cast on. With knitting needle and project yarn, pick up indicated number of sts in the "bumps" on back of chain. When indicated in pattern, "unzip" the crochet chain to free live sts.

PATTERN NOTES

When working crown of hat, change to double-pointed needles when stitches no longer fit comfortably on circular needle.

 Socks are worked from the toe top with short-row toe and heel.

 To make both socks match, divide 100g ball evenly into 2 [50g] balls, making sure that each ball begins at the same point in the color stripe sequence.

Hat

BODY

With circular needle and MC, cast on 90 sts; place marker for beg of rnd and join, taking care not to twist sts.

 Work 10 rnds in Wide Rib.
***Next rnd:** Change to CC and knit.
 Work 2 rnds Wide Rib.
Next rnd: Change to MC and knit.**
 Work 2 rnds in Wide Rib.
 Rep from * to ** once more.
 Continue in MC and Wide Rib until hat measures 6 inches.

CROWN

Next rnd: *K4, p2tog, k4, p2; rep from * around—82 sts.
Next rnd: *K4, p1, k4, p2tog; rep from * around—75 sts.
Next rnd: *K3, ssk; rep from * around—60 sts.
 Knit 2 rnds.
Next rnd: *K13, k2tog; rep from * around—56 sts.
Next rnd: *K5, k2tog, place marker; rep from * around—48 sts.
Next rnd: *Knit to 2 sts before marker, k2tog; rep from * around—40 sts.
 Rep last rnd 5 times, and remove markers on last rnd—8 sts.
 Cut yarn, leaving a 5-inch tail.
 Using tapestry needle, thread tail through rem sts, and pull tight.

FINISHING

Weave in all ends. Block as necessary.

Sock

TOE

Divide 100g of sock yarn into 2 equal parts of 50g each.

 Using provisional method, cast on 34 (38) sts.

*Row 1 (RS): Knit to last st, W&T.

Row 2: Purl to last st, W&T.

Row 3: Knit to 1 st before previously wrapped st, W&T.

Row 4: Purl to 1 st before previously wrapped st, W&T.

Rep Rows 3 and 4 until 11 (12) sts are wrapped at each side of the toe, leaving 12 (14) sts unwrapped in the center.

Row 5: Knit to first wrapped st, WW, W&T.

Row 6: Purl to first wrapped st, WW, W&T.

Row 7: Knit to double-wrapped st, WW, W&T.

Row 8: Knit to double-wrapped st, WW, W&T.

Rep Rows 7 and 8 until 2 double-wrapped sts rem (1 at each end).

Row 9: Knit across, WW**, place marker for beg of rnd; unzip Provisional Cast-On and distribute 34 (38) newly live (instep) sts and sole sts as follows: N1 and N2 (instep sts): 16 (19) sts each; N3 and N4 (sole sts): 18 (19) sts each—68 (76) sts.

FOOT

Rnd 1: Knit around, working last double-wrapped tog with st when you come to it.

Knit 4 rnds.

Set-up rnd: N1 and N2: [P2, k4] 5 (6) times, p2; N3 and N4: knit.

Work even with Wide Rib on instep sts and St st on sole sts until foot measures approx 9 (10) inches or approx 2 inches short of desired length.

HEEL

Size Small only

Sl 1 st from end of N3 to N2 and 1 st from end of N4 to N1—17 sts on each needle.

Both sizes

Working on sole sts only, work short-row heel as for toe from * to **.

LEG

Size Small only

Rnd 1: N1 and N2: Work Wide Rib as established; N3 and N4: continue around in established Wide Rib and dec 1 at beg of N3 and end of N4, working last double-wrapped st when you come to it—66 sts.

Size Large only

Rnd 1: N1 and N2: Work Wide Rib as established; N3 and N4: continue around in established Wide Rib and M1 at beg of N3 and end of N4, working new sts into pat and working last double-wrapped st when you come to it—78 sts.

Both Sizes

Continue in Wide Rib until sock measures 6 inches or desired length.

Bind off loosely in pat.

FINISHING

Weave in all ends. Wash and block to size. ✪

Honeycomb Cable Cap & Socks

This eye-catching cabled hat and sock ensemble is the perfect look for a cool autumn outing.

DESIGNS BY KARA GOTT WARNER

◼◼◼◻ INTERMEDIATE

SIZES
Hat: Adult average
Socks: Woman's small (large) to fit shoe sizes 5–7 (8–10) Instructions are given for smaller size, with larger size in parentheses. When only 1 number is given, it applies to both sizes.

FINISHED MEASUREMENTS
Hat circumference: 21 inches
Sock circumference: 8¼ (9¼) inches
Foot Length: 8¾ (10) inches

MATERIALS
- Colinette Cadenza (worsted weight; 100% merino wool; 131 yds/50g per skein): 2 skeins Raphael #70 (hat)
- Colinette Jitterbug (sock weight; 100% merino wool; 318 yds/110g per skein): 1 skein Raphael #70 (socks)
- Size 2 (3mm) 42-inch circular needle or size needed to obtain gauge (socks)
- Size 6 (4mm) double-pointed (set of 4) and 16-inch circular needles or size needed to obtain gauge (hat)
- Small crochet hook
- Stitch markers, 1 in CC for beg of rnd

GAUGE
Hat: 27 sts and 30 rnds= 4 inches/10cm in cable pat.
Socks: 27 sts and 40 rnds = 4 inches/10cm in St st.
To save time, take time to check gauge.

SPECIAL ABBREVIATIONS
Wrap and Turn (W&T): Bring yarn to RS of work between needles, slip next st pwise to RH needle, bring yarn around this st to WS, slip st back to LH needle, turn work to begin working back in the other direction.

Work wrapped sts and wraps tog (WW): *On RS:* Knit to wrapped st, slip the wrapped st pwise from LH needle to RH needle. Use tip of LH needle to pick up wrap(s) and place it/them on RH needle. Slip wrap(s) and st back to LH needle and knit them tog.

On WS: Purl to wrapped st, slip the wrapped st kwise from LH needle to RH needle. Use tip of LH to pick up wrap(s) and place it/them on RH needle. Slip wrap(s) and st back to LH needle and purl them tog.

PATTERN STITCHES
Hat Band Pat (multiple of 3 sts)
Rnd 1: Purl.
Rnds 2 and 3: K1, sl 1 wyif, k1.
Rnd 4: Knit.
Rep Rnds 1–4 for pat.

Honeycomb Cable
See chart.

Sock Cuff Pat (even number
of sts)
Rnd 1: *K1, sl 1 wyif; rep from * around.
Rnd 2: Knit.
　Rep Rnds 1 and 2 for pat.

SPECIAL TECHNIQUE

Provisional Cast-On: With crochet hook
and waste yarn, make a chain several
sts longer than desired cast on. With
knitting needle and project yarn, pick up
indicated number of sts in the "bumps"
on back of chain. When indicated in
pattern, "unzip" the crochet chain to free
live sts.

PATTERN NOTES

For cap, change to double-pointed
needles when stitches no longer fit
comfortably on circular needle.
　The socks are worked on 1 long circular
needle using the "Magic Loop" method
(page 12) from the toe up with short-row
toe and heel.

Hat

BAND

Cast on 126 sts; place marker for beg of
rnd and join, taking care not to twist sts.

Work 3 reps of Hat Band pat.
Inc rnd: *K6, k1 in front and back of next
st; rep from * around—144 sts.
　Beg and ending rep where indicated for
hat, work Honeycomb Cable chart twice
and on last rnd, place markers every 9 sts.

CROWN

Rnd 1 (dec): *Knit to 2 sts before marker,
k2tog; rep from * around—128 sts.
Rnd 2: Knit.
　Rep [Rnds 1 and 2] 4 times—64 sts.
　Rep Rnd 1 twice—32 sts.
Next rnd: Removing markers, k2tog
around—16 sts.
Next rnd: *K2, k2tog; rep from *
around—12 sts.
　Cut yarn, leaving a 6-inch tail.
　Using tapestry needle, thread tail
through rem sts, and pull tight and
secure to WS.

FINISHING

Weave in all ends. Block.

Socks

TOE

Using provisional method, cast on 26 (30)
sts.
Row 1 (WS): Purl.
Row 2: Knit to last 2 sts on needle, W&T.
Row 3: Purl to last 2 sts on needle, W&T.
Row 4: Knit to 1 st before wrapped st,
W&T.
Row 5: Purl to 1 st before wrapped st,
W&T.
　Rep Rows 4 and 5 until there are 10 (14)
unwrapped sts in center.
Row 6: Knit to wrapped st, WW, W&T.
Row 7: Purl to wrapped st, WW, W&T.
Row 8: Knit to double-wrapped st, WW,
W&T.
Row 9: Purl to double-wrapped st, WW,
W&T.

Rep Rows 8 and 9 until all wrapped sts are worked.
Last row: Knit to last wrapped st, WW.

FOOT

Remove waste yarn from cast on row and place the 26 (30) sts onto needle to beg working in the rnd.

Work Honeycomb Cable on first 26 (30) sts [instep], then work in St st on the next 30 sts [sole], working last double-wrap tog with st on first rnd.

Work even until piece measures 7¼ (8½) inches from beg of toe or approx 1½ inches short of desired length, ending on last rnd of cable pat, ready to begin working heel on sole sts.

HEEL

Work short-row heel on 26 (30) sole sts as for short-row toe.

LEG

Continue in pats as established all around (cable pat on front sock sts, St st on back sock sts).

Work 1 [15-rnd] rep of Honeycomb Cable.

CUFF

Purl 1 rnd.
Work Sock Cuff pat for ¾ inches.
Purl 1 rnd.

Bind off all sts very loosely using needle several sizes larger than working needle.

FINISHING

Weave in ends. Block lightly. ✪

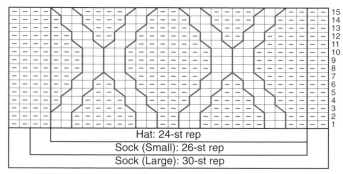

	15
	14
	13
	12
	11
	10
	9
	8
	7
	6
	5
	4
	3
	2
	1

Hat: 24-st rep
Sock (Small): 26-st rep
Sock (Large): 30-st rep

HONEYCOMB CABLE

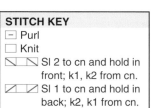

STITCH KEY
- Purl
- Knit
- Sl 2 to cn and hold in front; k1, k2 from cn.
- Sl 1 to cn and hold in back; k2, k1 from cn.

Sideways Striped Chuk & Socks

Hey, socks don't match! What clever way to use those bits of worsted weight yarn.

DESIGNS BY LOIS YOUNG

Hat: EASY

Socks: INTERMEDIATE

SIZES
Child's small (medium) Instructions are given for smaller size with larger size in parentheses. If only one number is given, it applies to both sizes.

FINISHED MEASUREMENTS
Hat circumference: 18 (20) inches
Hat height: 7½ (9) inches
Sock circumference: 6 (7) inches
Foot Length: 7 (8½) inches

MATERIALS
- Mission Falls 1824 Wool (worsted weight; 100% merino superwash; 85 yds/50g per ball): 2 balls each cocoa #007 (A), denim #021 (B), poppy #011 (C) and ink #022 (D) for set; 1 ball each if doing only hat or socks
- Size 7 (4.5 mm) double-pointed needles (set of 4) or size needed to obtain gauge (socks)
- Size 8 (5mm) 16-inch circular needle or size needed to obtain gauge (hat)
- Stitch markers

GAUGE
Hat: 18 sts and 36 rows = 4 inches/10cm in garter stitch with larger needle.
Socks: 20 sts and 26 rnds = 4 inches/10cm in St st with smaller needles.
To save time, take time to check gauge.

SPECIAL ABBREVIATIONS
N1, N2, N3: Needle 1, Needle 2, Needle 3

PATTERN STITCHES

Wedge 1
Rows 1 and 2: Using A or C, knit to end of row.
Row 3: Knit to last 10 sts, turn.
Rows 4, 6, 8, 10, 12: Sl 1, knit to end of row.
Row 5: Knit to last 8 sts, turn.
Row 7: Knit to last 6 sts, turn.
Row 9: Knit to last 4 sts, turn.
Row 11: Knit to last 2 sts, turn.
Rows 13 and 14: Rep Row 1.

Size Small only
Work Wedge 1 omitting Rows 3 and 4.

Wedge 2
Rows 1 and 2: Using B or D, knit to end of row.
Row 3: Knit to last 2 sts, turn.
Rows 4, 6, 8, 10, 12: Sl 1, knit to end of row.
Row 5: Knit to last 4 sts, turn.

Row 7: Knit to last 6 sts, turn.
Row 9: Knit to last 8 sts, turn.
Row 11: Knit to last 10 sts, turn.
Rows 13 and 14: Rep Row 1.

Size Small only
Work Wedge 2 omitting Rows 11 and 12.

PATTERN NOTES

"Chuk" is what a stocking cap is called in Michigan's Upper Peninsula. It is thought to have come from the French word "toque," denoting a hat.

The hat is worked sideways in a series of joined wedges with 1 seam. The brim is picked up along bottom edge and knit in the round.

The socks are worked from the cuff down on 3 double-pointed needles with a heel flap, gussets and wedge toe.

Hat

CROWN

With circular needle and A, cast on 27 (36) sts.

Using A, work Wedge 1, beg with Row 2.

Continue alternating Wedges 1 and 2, working colors in the following order: B, C, D, A. When 12 wedges have been worked, bind off on last row of last wedge.

With RS facing and A, pick up and knit 24 sts along top edge of hat, turn.
Row 1 (WS): K2tog around, turn—12 sts.
Row 2: K2tog around—6 sts.

Cut yarn leaving a 6-inch tail. Using tapestry needle, thread tail through 6 rem sts and fasten off.

Turn hat inside out and sew seam; thread tail through 6 top sts again and pull tight; secure to WS.

BRIM

With RS facing, using larger needle and A, pick up and knit 64 (72) sts evenly spaced around bottom of hat. Place marker for beg of rnd and join.

[Purl 1 rnd, knit 1 rnd] 3 times.
Loosely bind off pwise.

FINISHING

Weave in all ends. Block.

Socks

SOCK 1

With dpns and C, loosely cast on 30 (34) sts. Distribute evenly to 3 dpns, place marker for beg of rnd and join, taking

care not to twist sts.

Work in K1, P1 Rib until cuff measures 4½ (5) inches or desired length.

Cut C, leaving a 4-inch tail.

HEEL FLAP

Slip first 14 (16) sts to 1 dpn for heel, and divide rem 16 (18) sts on 2 other dpns to be kept on hold for instep.

Change to B.

Row 1 (RS): Working on heel sts only, sl 1, knit to end.

Row 2: Sl 1, purl to end.

Rep Rows 1 and 2 until 14 (16) rows have been worked.

TURN HEEL

Row 1: K7 (8), ssk, k1, turn.

Row 2: Sl 1, p1, p2tog, p1, turn.

Row 3: Sl 1, k3, ssk, k1, turn.

Row 4: Sl 1, p5, p2tog, p1, turn—8 sts.

Size Medium only

Row 5: Sl 1, k7, ssk, turn.

Row 6: Sl 1, p7, p2tog, turn—10 sts.

Cut B, leaving a 4-inch tail.

GUSSET

Change to A.

Set-up Rnd: N1: Beg at top of heel flap where instep and heel joins, pick up and knit 8 (9) sts along right edge of flap, k4 (5) heel sts; N2: k4 (5) heel sts, pick up and knit 8 (9) sts along left edge of flap; N3: k16 (18) instep sts, place marker for beg of rnd—40 (46) sts distributed as follows: N1: 12 (14) sts; N2: 12 (14) sts; N3: 16 (18) sts.

Rnd 1 (dec): N1: Ssk, knit to end; N2: knit to last 2 sts, k2tog; N3; knit—38 (44) sts.

Rnd 2: Work even.

Rep [Rnds 1 and 2] 5 (6) times—28 (32) sts.

FOOT

Work even until foot measures 5½ (6½) inches from back of heel.

Cut A, leaving a 4-inch tail.

TOE

Slip first st on N3 to N2 and last st on N3 to N1—7 (8) sts on N1 and N2 and 14 (16) sts on N3.

Change to D.

Rnd 1 (dec): N1: K1, ssk, knit to end; N2: knit to last 3 sts, k2tog, k1; N3: k1, ssk, knit to last 3 sts, k2tog, k1—24 (28) sts.

Rnd 2: Knit.

Rep Rnds 1 and 2 until 16 sts rem.

Rep Rnd 1 only, until 8 sts rem.

Cut yarn, leaving a 10-inch tail.

Slip sts on N1 to N2.

Graft toe using Kitchener St (page 17).

FINISHING

Weave in all ends, using tails at beg of heel flap to close and tighten holes that may appear.

SOCK 2

Work as for Sock 1, but reverse the order of the colors as follows: D, A, B, C. ✪

Pixie Stocking Cap & Booties

Spread a little "pixie dust" with this enchanting bootie and cap ensemble.

DESIGNS BY ERSSIE MAJOR

■■■□ INTERMEDIATE

SIZES

Infant's 0–3 (3–6, 6–9, 9–12, 12–18) months Instructions are given for smallest size, with larger sizes in parentheses. When only 1 number is given, it applies to all sizes.

FINISHED MEASUREMENTS

Hat circumference: 13¾ (14½, 16, 16¾, 17½) inches
Hat length: 13 (15¼, 17, 21, 24¼) inches (excluding pompom)
Bootie circumference: 4¼ (5, 5¾, 6½, 7¼) inches
Foot length: 3½ (3¾, 4, 4¼, 4¾) inches

MATERIALS

- Colinette Cadenza (DK weight; 100% merino wool; 131 yds/50g per hank): 2 (2, 3, 3, 3) hanks in Mardi Gras #155

  3 LIGHT
- Size 6 (4mm) double-pointed needles (set of 5) or size needed to obtain gauge.
- Stitch marker
- Pieces of cardboard (or pompom maker)
- 1 jingle bell

GAUGE

22 sts and 28 rnds = 4 inches/10cm in St st.
To save time, take time to check gauge.

SPECIAL ABBREVIATIONS

N1, N2, N3, N4: Needle 1, Needle 2, Needle 3, Needle 4
Wrap and Turn (W&T): Bring yarn to RS of work between needles, slip next st pwise to RH needle, bring yarn around this st to WS, slip st back to LH needle, turn work to begin working back in the other direction.
Work wrapped sts and wraps tog (WW): *On RS:* Knit to wrapped st, slip the wrapped st pwise from LH needle to RH needle. Use tip of LH needle to pick up wrap(s) and place it/them on RH needle. Slip wrap(s) and st back to LH needle and knit them tog.
  On WS: Purl to wrapped st, slip the wrapped st kwise from LH needle to RH needle. Use tip of LH to pick up wrap(s) and place it/them on RH needle. Slip wrap(s) and st back to LH needle and purl them tog.

PATTERN NOTES

The socks are worked from the cuff down on 4 double-pointed needles with a picot hem, short-row heel and wedge toe.
  N1 and N2 hold heel/sole stitches; N3 and N4 hold instep stitches.

Pixie Hat

HEM

Cast on 76 (80, 88, 92, 96) sts and

of the other 3 needles—68 (72, 80, 84, 88) sts.

Knit 8 (10, 10, 12, 14) rnds.

Rep from ** until 12 (16, 16, 12, 16) sts rem.

Cut yarn, leaving a 5-inch tail.

Using tapestry needle, thread tail through rem sts, and pull tight.

Cut two cardboard circles each 2 inches in diameter. Cut a hole in the center of each circle, about ½-inch in diameter. Thread a tapestry needle with a length of yarn doubled. Holding both circles together, insert needle through center hole, over the outside edge, through center again until entire circle is covered and center hole is filled (thread more length of yarn as needed). With sharp scissors, cut yarn between the two circles all around the circumference. Using two 12-inch strands of yarn, slip yarn between circles and overlap yarn ends 2 or 3 times to prevent knot from slipping, pull tightly and tie into a firm knot. Remove cardboard and fluff pompom by rolling it between your hands. Trim even with scissors, leaving tying ends for attaching pompom to project.

Attach pompom to top of hat, then take yarn ends to WS to attach a small jingle bell to the inside of the hat. Be careful to secure the bell so that it cannot be taken off by a baby's fingers.

Pixie Booties

CUFF

Cast on 24 (28, 32, 36, 40) sts and distribute evenly on 4 dpns with 6 (7, 8, 9, 10) sts on each dpn; place marker for beg of rnd and join, taking care not to twist sts.

Knit 6 rnds.

Next rnd (picot turning edge): *Yo,

distribute evenly among 4 dpns with 19 (20, 22, 23, 24) sts on each dpn; place marker for beg of rnd and join, taking care not to twist sts.

Knit 6 rnds.

Next rnd (picot turning edge): *Yo, k2tog rep from * around.

Knit 6 rnds.

Next rnd (joining rnd): With LH needle, pick up first cast on st, then knit it tog with first st of rnd, *pick up next cast on st and knit it tog with next st; rep from * around, joining hem.

BODY

Work even in St st until piece measures 3¾ (4, 4¼, 4¼, 4½) inches from picot turning edge.

CROWN

Dec rnd: *K1, k2tog, knit to last 3 sts on first needle, ssk, k1; rep from * on each

k2tog; rep from * around.

Knit 6 rnds.

Next rnd (joining rnd): With LH needle, pick up first cast-on st, then knit it tog with first st of rnd, *pick up next cast-on st and knit it tog with next st; rep from * around, joining hem. Knit 8 (10, 10, 12, 12) rnds.

Purl 1 rnd (turning rnd).

Turn work and start working rnd in opposite direction so that WS becomes RS and cuff folds back on purl edge.

LEG

Knit 15 (17, 17, 19, 19) rnds.

Next rnd: *K2, yo, k2tog; rep from * around.

Knit 5 rnds.

HEEL

Slip sts on N2 to N1 for heel, leaving rem sts on hold on N3 and N4 for instep.

Row 1 (RS): Working on heel sts only, knit to last st, W&T.

Row 2: Purl to last st, W & T.

Row 3: Knit to 1 st before previously wrapped st, W&T.

Row 4: Purl 1 st before previously wrapped st, W&T.

Rep Rows 3 and 4 until 4 (4, 5, 6, 6) sts are wrapped on each side of the toe, leaving 4 (6, 6, 6, 8) sts unwrapped in the center.

Row 5: Knit to first wrapped st, WW, W&T.

Row 6: Purl to first wrapped st, WW, W&T.

Row 7: Knit to first double-wrapped st, WW, W&T.

Row 8: Purl to first double-wrapped st, WW, W&T.

Rep Rows 7 and 8 until all sts have been worked and 1 double-wrapped st rem at each end.

FOOT

Rnd 1: With N1, k6 (7, 8, 9, 10); with N2, knit to double-wrapped st, WW; with N3 and N4: knit across, place marker for beg

of rnd.

Rnd 2: WW last double-wrapped st, knit around.

Work even in St st until foot measures approx 2¾ (3, 3¼, 3½, 4) inches or ¾ inch short of desired length.

TOE

Dec rnd: N1: K1, ssk, knit to end; N2: knit to last 3 sts, k2tog, k1; N3 and N4: work as for N1 and N2—20 (24, 26, 32, 36) sts.

Rep Dec rnd until 8 sts rem.

Graft sole and instep sts using Kitchener st (see page 17).

TWISTED CORDS

Cut 3 strands each 1 yd long. Fold in half, tie ends tog, and secure folded end to a stationary object. Twist yarn until it begins to double back on itself. Fold in half again with both ends together and allow to twist upon itself. Tie a knot a short way from each end, then cut end to make a small tassel. Tie 2 more knots on either side of the center of the cord, then cut between these 2 knots, resulting in 2 twisted cords.

Thread each cord through eyelets on each of the booties and tie bows at front. Weave in all ends. ✪

Kirsten Cap & Sockies

This delightful duo features accent picot edging and contrasting yarns, creating eye-catching results.

DESIGNS BY PATTI PIERCE STONE

◼◼◼◻ INTERMEDIATE

SIZES

Infant/Child's (3–6, 6–9, 9–12, 12–18) months to fit infant's shoe size 1 (3, 4, 5, 8) Instructions are given for smallest size, with larger sizes in parentheses. When only 1 number is given, it applies to all sizes.

FINISHED MEASUREMENT

Hat circumference: 13½ (14¼, 15, 15¾, 16½) inches

MATERIALS

- Tahki•Stacy Charles Cotton Classic (DK weight; 100% mercerized cotton; 108 yds/50g per skein): 1 (2, 2, 2, 3) skeins lavender #3936 (MC) and 1 skein white #3001 (CC)
- Size 3 (3.25mm) 24-inch circular needle and spare needle (of any sort) or size needed to obtain gauge [socks]
- Size 4 (3.5mm) 29-inch (or longer) circular needle and spare needle (of any sort) [hat and socks]
- Size 6 (4mm) 29-inch (or longer) circular needle or size needed to obtain gauge [hat]
- Size E/4 (3.5mm) crochet hook
- Stitch markers, 1 in CC for beg of rnd

GAUGE

Hat: 22 sts and 28 rnds = 4 inches/10cm in St st using size 6 needle.
Socks: 23 sts and 29 rnds = 4 inches/10cm in St st using size 3 needle.

To save time, take time to check gauge.

SPECIAL TECHNIQUE

Provisional Cast-On: With crochet hook and waste yarn, make a chain several sts longer than desired cast on. With knitting needle and project yarn, pick up indicated number of sts in the "bumps" on back of chain. When indicated in pattern, "unzip" the crochet chain to free live sts.

PATTERN NOTES

The patterns for both the hat and the sockies are written so that the project is knit on one circular needle using the "Magic Loop" method (page 12). You can opt to work on double-pointed or 2 circular needles.

The socks are worked from the top down with a picot hem, semi-wrapped short-row heel and wedge toe.

When working the semi-wrapped short-row heel, slip first stitch of each row purlwise with yarn in back.

Hat

PICOT HEM

Using provisional method, smaller hat needle and MC, cast on 72 (76, 80, 84, 88) sts; distribute sts as for Magic Loop; place marker for beg of rnd and join, being

careful not to twist sts.

Knit 6 rnds.

Turning rnd: K1, *yo, k2tog; rep from * to last st, end yo, knit last st on rnd tog with first st on next rnd.

Knit 6 rnds.

Join hem: **Unzip waste yarn from approx 25 percent of Provisional Cast-On sts; slip live sts to spare needle the same size as main needle; holding the 2 needles parallel with RS of fabric facing and using larger needle and CC, *knit tog 1 st from each needle, yo; rep from * to last st on spare needle, then rep from ** until all cast on sts are used up. Slip first st

of next rnd to RH needle so that next rnd beg with yo—144 (152, 160, 168, 176) sts.

Next rnd: P2tog around, cut CC—72 (76, 80, 84, 88) sts.

BODY

With MC and larger needle, knit every rnd until hat measures 2 (3, 3¼, 3¾, 3¾) inches from picot edge, or 2 (2¼, 2½, 2½, 2 ¾) inches short of desired length.

CROWN

Note: *On following rnd place markers following each dec.*

Rnd 1 (0–3 months): [K12, k3tog, k12, k2tog] twice, k12, k2tog—65 sts.

Rnd 1 (3–6 months): K13, k3tog, [k13, k2tog] 4 times—70 sts.

Rnd 1 (6–9 months): [K14, k2tog] 5 times—75 sts.

Rnd 1 (9–12 months): [K14, k3tog] 4 times, k14, k2tog—75 sts.

Rnd 1 (12–18 months): [K15, k2tog, k15, k3tog] twice, k15, k3tog—80 sts.

Rnd 2: Knit.

Dec rnd: Slipping markers, *knit to 2 sts before marker, p2tog; rep from * around—60 (65, 70, 70, 75) sts.

Rep Dec rnd [every other rnd] 8 times, then every rnd until 20 sts rem.

Last rnd: K2tog around—10 sts.

Cut yarn, leaving an 8-inch tail. Using tapestry needle, thread tail through rem sts, and pull tight. Secure on WS.

EARFLAPS

Earflaps are worked flat over 12 sts on opposite sides of the hat.

With RS facing and using larger needle, count 12 (13, 14, 15, 16) sts to the left from center back of hat (at cast on tail). Place marker or piece of waste yarn, so the placement can be seen from the inside of the hat. Rep, working to the right from the center back marker. This notes the placement of the ear flaps.

Turn hat inside out.

With larger hat needle, beg at the left marker, pick up 12 sts in the back side of sts in the picot joining row, working toward the front of the hat. Attach MC.

Rows 1, 3, 5 (WS): K2, purl to last 2 sts, sl 2 pwise wyif.

Row 2 (RS): Knit to last 2 sts, sl 2 pwise wyif.

Row 4: K3, [yo, ssk, p1] twice, k1, sl 2 pwise wyif.

Row 6: K3, [k2tog, yo, p1] twice, k1, sl 2 pwise wyif.

Row 7: Rep Row 1.

Rows 8–13: Rep Rows 4–7, then Rows 4 and 5.

Row 14: K3, [k2tog, p1] twice, k1, sl 2 pwise wyif—10 sts.

Row 15: Rep Row 1.

Row 16: K3, ssk, k2tog, k1, sl 2 pwise wyif—8 sts.

Row 17: K2, p2tog, p2tog-tbl, sl 2 pwise wyif—6 sts.

Row 18: K1, k2tog, k2tog, k1—4 sts.

Cut yarn, leaving a 6-inch tail.

With RS facing and using tapestry needle, thread tail through rem sts from right to left; secure to WS of edge.

Weave in all ends.

Make another earflap, beg at the marker on the opposite side of the hat.

of next sl st; rep from * around.

Cut MC. Weave in all ends. Sew 1 flower to top of hat and other 2 flowers to ends of cord.

Sockies

Using provisional method, smaller sock needle and MC, cast on 24 (26, 28, 32, 34) sts, distribute sts evenly as for Magic Loop (heel sts on first needle tip, instep sts on 2nd needle tip); place marker for beg of rnd and join, being careful not to twist sts.

Knit 4 rnds.

Turning rnd: K1, *yo, k2tog; rep from * to last st, end yo, knit last st on rnd tog with first st on next rnd.

Knit 4 rnds.

Join hem: **Unzip waste yarn from approx 25 percent of Provisional Cast-On sts; slip live sts to spare needle the same size as main needle; holding the 2 needles parallel with RS of fabric facing and using larger needle and CC, *knit tog 1 st from each needle, yo; rep from * to last st on dpn, then rep from ** until all cast on sts are used up. Slip first st of next rnd to RH needle so that next rnd beg with yo.

Next rnd: P2tog around, cut CC—24 (26, 28, 32, 34) sts.

LEG

With MC and larger needle, work in St st until piece measures 2 (2¼, 2½, 2¾, 3) inches from picot edge or to desired length to top of heel. Cut MC.

SEMI-WRAPPED SHORT ROW HEEL

Note: Short rows are worked back and forth on heel sts only.

Row 1: Join CC and knit across heel sts, turn.

Row 2: Sl 1, purl to last st, k1, turn.

Row 3: Sl 1, k10 (11, 12, 14, 15), turn.

Row 4: Sl 1, p8 (9, 10, 12, 13), k1, turn.

TWISTED CORD

Make 2

Cut 2 strands 3 yds long (or approx 6 times desired length). Fold in half, tie ends tog with a loose overhand knot and secure folded end to a stationary object.

Twist yarn until it begins to double back on itself. Fold in half again with both ends tog and allow to twist up on itself.

Cut to desired length (if necessary) and knot the ends to secure.

Sew 1 end to each earflap.

CROCHETED FLOWER

Make 3

Rnd 1: With CC, ch 2. Work 9 sc in 2nd ch from hook; sl st in top of first sc to join. Cut CC.

Rnd 2: Attach MC in the top of any st, [ch 4, skip next st, sl st in the top of the next st] 4 times, ch 4, sl st in top of the first sl st to join.

Rnd 3: *3 hdc in next ch-4 sp, sl st in top

Row 5: Sl 1, k8 (9, 10, 12, 13), turn.
Row 6: Sl 1, p6 (7, 8, 10, 11), k1, turn.
Row 7: Sl 1, k6 (7, 8, 10, 11), turn.
Row 8: Sl 1, p4 (5, 6, 8, 9), k1, turn.
 Continue with Heel Turn.
Sizes 9–12 and 12–18 months only
Row 9: Sl 1, k8 (9), turn.
Row 10: Sl 1, p6 (7), k1, turn.
 Continue with Heel Turn.

HEEL TURN

Row 1: Sl 1, k5 (6, 7, 7, 8); insert the tip of the LH needle into the purl bump at the edge of the RH previous row and k2tog-tbl with next st, turn.
Row 2: Sl 1, p6 (7, 8, 8, 9); insert the tip of the LH needle into the purl bump at the edge of the RH previous row and p2tog with next st, turn.
Row 3: Sl 1, k7 (8, 9, 9, 10); pick up the purl bump as before (this one, and all the rest, will be 2 rows down) and k2tog-tbl with next st, turn.
Row 4: Sl 1, p8 (9, 10, 10, 11); pick up the purl bump and p2tog, turn.
Row 5: Sl 1, k9 (10, 11, 11, 12); pick up the purl bump and k2tog-tbl; turn.
 Continue in this manner until all heel sts have been worked.
Last heel row: Sl 1, knit across heel sts; pick up running thread between very first heel st and first instep st and place on LH needle; pick up the purl bump from the last st on the heel rnd (now 2 rows below) and place on LH needle; knit running thread and the purl bump tog tbl. Cut CC.
Joining rnd: With MC, knit across instep sts; with RH needle, pick up running thread between last instep st and first heel st; pick up the purl bump from the first heel st on the rnd (now 2 rows below) and place on RH needle; work running thread and the purl bump tog as ssk; knit across heel sts—26 (28, 30, 34, 36) sts distributed as follows: 12 (13, 14, 16, 17) instep sts; 14 (15, 16, 18, 19) heel/sole sts.

FOOT

Work in St st until foot measures 4 (4½, 5, 5½, 6) inches from back of heel or ¾ (¾, 1, 1, 1, 1¼) inches short of desired length. Cut MC.

TOE

Rnd 1: With CC, work both instep and sole sts as follows: K1, ssk, knit to last 3 sts, k2tog, k1—22 (24 26, 30, 32) sts.
Rnd 2: Knit around.
 Rep Rnds 1 and 2 until 6 (7, 8, 8, 9) instep sts and 8 (9, 10, 10, 11) sole sts rem.
Last rnd: Instep sts: knit across; sole sts: k1, ssk, knit to last 3 sts, k2tog, k1—12 (14, 16, 16, 18) sts.
 Weave toe sts tog using Kitchener st (see page 17).

FINISHING

Weave in all ends. Block as desired. ✪

General Information

BASIC STITCHES
Garter Stitch
When working back and forth, knit every row. When working in the round on circular or double-pointed needles, knit one round then purl one round.

Stockinette Stitch
When working back and forth, knit right-side rows and purl wrong-side rows. When working in the round on circular or double-pointed needles, knit all rounds.

Reverse Stockinette Stitch
When working back and forth, purl right-side rows and knit wrong-side rows. When working in the round on circular or double-pointed needles, purl all rounds.

Ribbing
Ribbing combines knit and purl stitches within a row to give stretch to the garment. Ribbing is most often used for cuffs of hats or socks, but may be used for the entire piece.

The rib pattern is established on the first row. On subsequent rows the knit stitches are knitted and purl stitches are purled to form the ribs.

READING PATTERN INSTRUCTIONS
Before beginning a pattern, read through it to make sure you are familiar with the abbreviations that are used.

Some patterns may be written for more than one size. In this case the smallest size is given first, and others are placed in parentheses. When only one number is given, it applies to all sizes.

You may wish to highlight the numbers for the size you are making before beginning. It is also helpful to place a self-adhesive sheet on the pattern to note any changes made while working the pattern.

MEASURING
To measure pieces, lay them flat on a smooth surface. To measure pieces, lay them flat on a smooth surface. Take the measurement in the middle of the piece, not along the outer edge where the edges tend to curve or roll.

GAUGE
The single most important factor in determining the finished size of a knit item is the gauge. Although not as important for flat, one-piece items, it is critical when making a clothing item that needs to fit properly.

It is important to make a stitch gauge swatch of at least 4 inches square with the recommended stitch patterns and needles before beginning.

Block the swatch, then measure it. If the number of stitches and rows in 4 inches are fewer than indicated under "Gauge" in the pattern, your needles are too large. Try another swatch with smaller-size needles. If the number of stitches and rows are more than indicated under "Gauge" in the pattern, your needles are too small. Try another swatch with larger-size needles.

Continue to adjust needles until correct gauge is achieved.

WORKING FROM CHARTS

When working with more than one color in a row, sometimes a chart is provided to help follow the pattern. On the chart each square represents one stitch. A key is given indicating the color or stitch represented by each color or symbol in the box.

When working in rows, odd-numbered rows are usually read from right to left and even-numbered rows from left to right.

For color-work charts, rows beginning at the right represent the right side of the work and are usually knit. Rows beginning at the left represent the wrong side and are usually purled.

When working in rounds, every row on the chart is a right-side row, and is read from right to left.

USE OF ZERO

In patterns that include various sizes, zeros are sometimes necessary. For example, k0 (0, 1) means if you are making the smallest or middle size, you would do nothing, and if you are making the largest size, you would k1.

Glossary

bind off—used to finish an edge

cast on—process of making foundation stitches used in knitting

decrease—means of reducing the number of stitches in a row

increase—means of adding to the number of stitches in a row

intarsia—method of knitting a multicolored pattern into the fabric

knitwise—insert needle into stitch as if to knit

make 1—method of increasing using the strand between the last stitch worked and the next stitch

place marker—placing a purchased marker or loop of contrasting yarn onto the needle for ease in working a pattern repeat

purlwise—insert needle into stitch as if to purl

right side—side of garment or piece that will be seen when worn

selvage (selvedge) stitch—edge stitch used to make seaming easier

slip, slip, knit—method of decreasing by moving stitches from left needle to right needle and working them together

slip stitch—an unworked stitch slipped from left needle to right needle, usually as if to purl

wrong side—side that will be inside when garment is worn

work even—continue to work in the pattern as established without working any increases or decreases

work in pattern as established—continue to work following the pattern stitch as it has been set up or established on the needle, working any increases or decreases in such a way that the established pattern remains the same

yarn over—method of increasing by wrapping the yarn over the right needle without working a stitch

Stranded or Fair Isle Knitting (2-Colors)

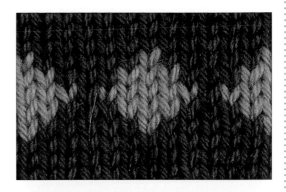

Changing colors of yarn within the row is called Stranded or Fair Isle knitting. This type of knitting can be worked either with both yarns in one hand or with one yarn in each hand. Carry the yarns along the wrong side of the fabric, working each color in the order indicated by the pattern. One color should always be carried under the other, whether you are knitting or purling—the strands will run parallel on the wrong side. They should never change positions; if they do, it will be apparent on the right side of the fabric. Carry both yarns to the end of each row and "lock" them in position on the last stitch.

When one of the yarns is carried across the back for more than 5 stitches (or about an inch), the yarn should be caught into the back of one of the stitches that is worked with the other yarn. This will prevent snags caused by long floats.

Fair Isle knitting creates a denser fabric than plain Stockinette knitting. Always work your gauge swatch in pattern before beginning your project. Watch your tension, ensuring that the stranded yarn is not pulled too tight; this will create puckers on the front of the fabric.

Intarsia

In certain patterns there are larger areas of color within the piece. Since this type of pattern requires a new color only for that section, it is not necessary to carry the yarn back and forth across the back. For this type of color change, a separate ball of yarn or bobbin is used for each color, making the yarn available only where needed. Bring the new yarn being used up-and-around the yarn just worked; this will "lock" the colors and prevent holes from occurring at the join.

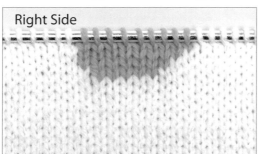

Right Side

Wrong Side

Seam Finishes

MATTRESS SEAM

This type of seam can be used for vertical seams (like side seams). It is worked with the right sides of the pieces facing you, making it easier to match stitches for stripe patterns. It is worked between the first and second stitch at the edge of the piece and works best when the first stitch is a selvage stitch.

To work this seam, thread a tapestry needle with matching yarn. Insert the needle into one corner of work from back to front, just above the cast on stitch, leaving a 3-inch tail. Take needle to edge of other piece and bring it from back to front at the corner of this piece.

Return to the first piece and insert the needle from the right to wrong side where the thread comes out of the piece. Slip the needle upward under two horizontal threads and bring the needle through to the right side.

Cross to the other side and repeat the same process "down where you came out, under two threads and up."

Continue working back and forth on the two pieces in the same manner for about an inch, then gently pull on the thread pulling the two pieces together. (Photo A)

Complete the seam and fasten off. Use the beginning tail to even-up the lower edge by working a figure 8 between the cast-on stitches at the corners. Insert the threaded needle from front to back under both threads of the corner cast-on stitch on the edge opposite the tail, then into the same stitch on the first edge. Pull gently until the figure 8 fills the gap. (Photo B)

When a project is made with a textured yarn that will not pull easily through the pieces, it is recommended that a smooth yarn of the same color be used to work the seam.

GARTER STITCH SEAMS

The "bumps" of the garter stitch selvage nestle between each other in a garter stitch seam, often producing a nearly reversible seam. This is a good seam for afghan strips and blocks of the same color. Starting as for the mattress seam, work from bump to bump, alternating sides. In this case you enter each stitch only once.

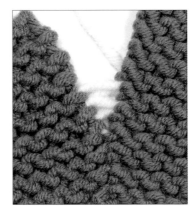

MATCHING PATTERNS

When it comes to matching stripes and other elements in a design, a simple formula makes things line up perfectly:

Begin the seam in the usual way.

Enter the first stitch of each new color stripe (or pattern detail) on the same side as you began the seam; i.e. the same side as your tail.

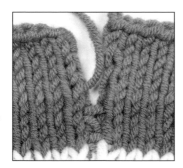

3-NEEDLE BIND OFF

Use this technique for seaming two edges together, such as when joining a seam. Hold the live edge stitches on two separate needles with right sides of the fabric together.

With a third needle, knit together a stitch from the front needle with one from the back.

Repeat, knitting a stitch from the front needle with one from the back needle once more.

Slip the first stitch over the second.

Repeat knitting, a front and back pair of stitches together, then bind one pair off.

Knitting with Beads

Threading beads onto yarn is the most common way to knit with beads.

Step 1: Before beginning to knit, thread half of the beads onto your skein of yarn using a bead threader. (These will be used for the first sock, the other half of the beads will be for the second sock.) As you work, unwind a small quantity of yarn, each time sliding the beads towards the ball until needed. Pass the yarn through the loop of the threader and pick up beads with the working end of the needle.

Step 2: Slide the beads over the loop and onto the yarn.

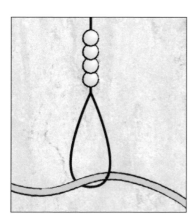

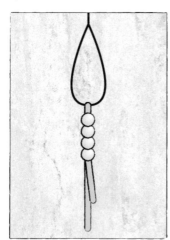

Knitting Basics

KNIT (K)

With yarn in back, insert tip of right needle from front to back in next stitch on left needle.

Bring yarn counterclockwise around the tip of the right needle.

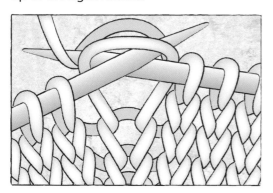

Pull yarn loop through the stitch with right needle point.

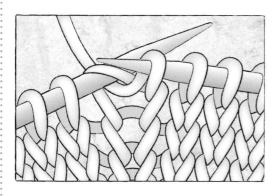

Slide the stitch off the left needle. The new stitch is on the right needle.

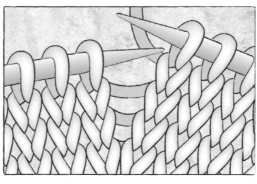

PURL (P)

With yarn in front, insert tip of right needle from back to front through front loop of the next stitch on the left needle.

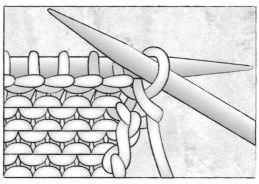

Bring yarn around the right needle counterclockwise.

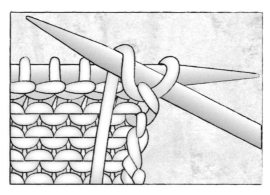

With right needle, draw yarn back through the stitch.

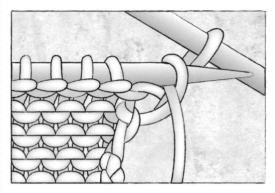

Slide the stitch off the left needle. The new stitch is on the right needle.

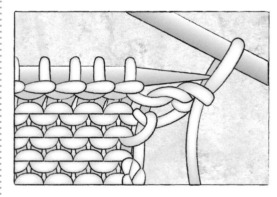

INCREASE (INC)
Two stitches in one stitch
Increase (knit)

Knit the next stitch in the usual manner, but don't remove the stitch from the left needle.

Place right needle behind left needle and knit again into the back of the same stitch. Slip original stitch off left needle.

Increase (purl)

Purl the next stitch in the usual manner, but don't remove the stitch from the left needle.

Place right needle behind left needle and purl again into the back of the same stitch. Slip original stitch off left needle.

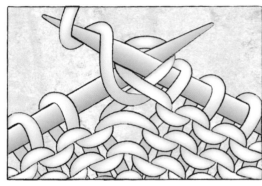

MAKE 1 INCREASE (M1)
Invisible Increase

Insert left needle from front to back under the horizontal loop between the last stitch worked and next stitch on left needle.

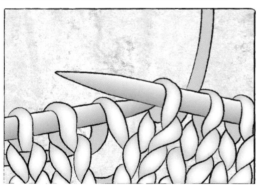

With right needle, knit into the back of this loop.

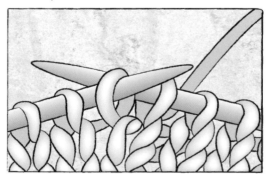

Backward Loop Increase over the right needle

With your thumb, make a loop over the right needle.

Slip the loop from your thumb onto the needle and pull to tighten.

Make 1 Increase in top of stitch below

Insert tip of right needle into the stitch on left needle one row below.

Knit this stitch, then knit the stitch on the left needle.

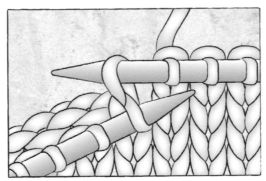

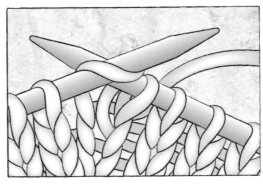

DECREASE (DEC)
Knit 2 together (k2tog)
Put tip of right needle through next two stitches on left needle as to knit. Knit these two stitches as one.

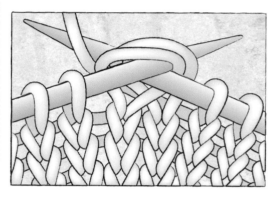

Purl 2 together (p2tog)
Put tip of right needle through next two stitches on left needle as to purl. Purl these two stitches as one.

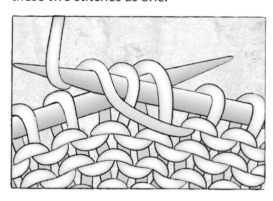

Slip, Slip, Knit (ssk)
Slip next two stitches, one at a time, as if to knit from left needle to right needle.

Insert left needle in front of both stitches and knit them together as one.

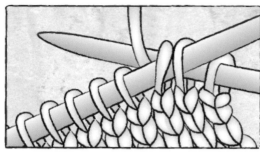

Slip, Slip, Purl (ssp)
Slip next two stitches, one at a time, as if to knit from left needle to right needle. Slip these stitches back onto left needle keeping them twisted.

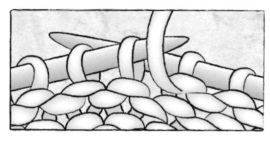

Purl these two stitches together through back loops.

Crochet Basics

Some knit items are finished with a crochet trim or edging. Below are some abbreviations used in crochet and a review of some basic crochet stitches.

CHAIN STITCH (CH)

Begin by making a slip knot on the hook. Bring the yarn over the hook from back to front and draw through the loop on the hook.

For each additional chain stitch, bring the yarn over the hook from back to front and draw through the loop on the hook.

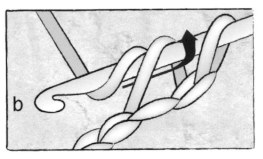

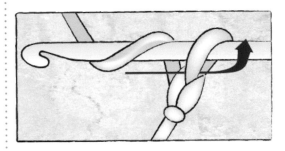

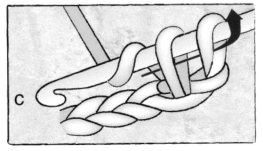

HALF DOUBLE CROCHET (HDC)

Yo, insert hook in st, yo, pull through st, yo, pull through all 3 lps on hook.

SINGLE CROCHET (SC)

Insert the hook in the second chain through the center of the V. Bring the yarn over the hook from back to front. Draw the yarn through the chain stitch and onto the hook.

Again bring yarn over the hook from back to front and draw it through both loops on hook.

For additional rows of single crochet, insert the hook under both loops of the previous stitch instead of through the center of the V as when working into the chain stitch.

SLIP STITCH (SL ST)

Insert hook under both loops of the stitch, bring yarn over the hook from back to front and draw it through the stitch and the loop on the hook.

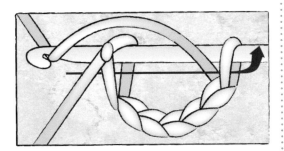

Special Thanks

We would like to thank the talented designers whose work is featured in this collection.

Laura Andersson
Wee Baby Bamboozle Hat & Socks, 125
Tiger-Striped Toque, 71
Orange You My Baby, 133

Kate Atherley
Fancy Fair Isle Socks, 87
Simple Self-Striping Socks, 137

Kathryn Beckerdite
Twisted Rib "Reversi" Socks, 105

Ellen Edwards Drechsler
Arctic Ear Flap Cap, 43
Simple Self-Striping Skullcap, 137

Nazanin S. Fard
Little Tike Toe-Up Socks, 109

Erika Flory
Corkscrew Tam, 39
Funky Chunky Cloche, 35

Julie Gaddy
All Buttoned Up Beanie, 25

Faina Goberstein
Twisted Rib Cap, 61

Kara Gott Warner
Twisted Basket Weave Newsboy, 67
Honeycomb Cable Cap & Socks, 145

Sean Higgins
Bahama Mama Flip-Flop Socks, 101

Amy Marie Marshall
Three Times a Delight, 119

Erssie Major
Itty Bitty Buggie Preemie Caps, 29
Man's Racing Stripe Cap & Socks, 141

Pixie Stocking Cap & Booties, 153
Three-Toned Topper, 49

Laura Nelkin
Walking Spiral Hat & Socks, 129
Cozy Cabled Leg Warmer, 115

Celeste Pinheiro
Bobble Lace Beanie, 51
Lacy Chain-Link Cable Head & Neck Warmer, 45
Nordic Tasseled Tam, 55
Sassy Swirl Hat, 33

Susan Robicheau
Tickle Your Toes Top-Down Socks, 91

Joanne Seiff
Playful Polka Dot Socks, 77

Ann Squire
Spring Has Sprung Hat, 23

Patti Pierce Stone
Kirsten Cap & Sockies, 157

Jennifer Tallapaneni
Phaidros Grecian Hat, 37

Ellene Warren
Electric Flower Socks, 85
Foot Fetish Socks, 93

Sarah Wilson
Daisy Rib Buttoned Leg Warmers, 111
Diamond Swirl Socks, 81
Zany Zigzag Socks, 97

Lois Young
Segmented Scandinavian Cloche, 63
Sideways Striped Chuk & Socks, 149

Diane Zangl
Plush Stripes Hat, 57

Yarn Resources

Many of the yarns presented in this book are available in your local yarn shop. If you should have any problems purchasing the yarns in your area, the list below will serve as a helpful resource.

Brown Sheep Company
800-826-9136
www.brownsheep.com

Cascade Yarns
206-574-0440
www.cascadeyarns.com

Classic Elite
800-444-5648
www.classicelite.com

Colinette (Unique Kolours, Inc.)
800-25-2dye4 (800-252-3934)
www.uniquekolours.com

Crystal Palace Yarns
510-237-9988
www.straw.com

Debbie Bliss (Knitting Fever)
(516) 546-3600
www.knittingfever.com

Knit Picks
800-574-1323
www.knitpicks.com

Koigu Wool Designs
888-765-9665
www.koigu.com

Mission Falls
877-244-1204
www.missionfalls.com

**Nashua Handknits
(Westminster Fibers)**
800-445-9276
www.westminsterfibers.com

Patons
888-368-8401
www.patonsyarns.com

Plymouth Yarn
215-788-0459
www.plymouthyarn.com

Premier Yarns
704-786-1155
www.premieryarns.com

Schaefer Yarn Company, Ltd.
607-532-9452
www.schaeferyarn.com

Skacel
(800) 255-1278
www.skacelknitting.com

Tahki Stacy Charles, Inc.
800-338-YARN (9276)
www.tahkistacycharles.com

Photo Index
Tops

23

25

29

33

35

37

39

43

45

49

51

55

57

61

63

67

71

Toes

81

77

85

91

87

93

101

97

105

11

109

115

Sets

119

129

125

133

137

141

145

149

153

157